Introduction to Microcomputer Programming

PETER C. SANDERSON, MA

Senior Advisory Officer (Computers),
Local Authorities Management
Services and Computer Committee

NEWNES TECHNICAL BOOKS

Newnes Technical Books

is an imprint of the Butterworth Group
which has principal offices in
London, Sydney, Toronto, Wellington, Durban and Boston

First published 1980
Reprinted 1981

British Library Cataloguing in Publication Data

Sanderson, Peter Crawshaw
    Introduction to microcomputer programming.
    1. Minicomputers — Programming
    I. Title
001.6'42   QA76.6   79-42861
ISBN 0-408-00415-0

Typeset by Butterworths Litho Preparation Department
Printed in England by Nene Litho, Earls Barton, Northants.
Bound by Weatherby Woolnough, Wellingborough, Northants.

Preface

The development of microprocessor-based computer systems has demolished the price barrier that hitherto inhibited computer usage. The use of a computer system is now feasible for a wide range of new users, especially small businesses, teachers and hobbyists. Yet, although systems are cheap, they are useless without programs. Commissioning a special program for individual use is expensive; a suite of business programs is likely to be more costly than the microcomputer system itself. On the other hand, using a 'package' program confines the user within the straitjacket created by the concepts of the program supplier. Many applications for businessman and hobbyist alike are so individual that a package solution would be inappropriate and inadequate. Sooner or later, most users of microcomputer systems will have to consider writing some of their own programs if they are to obtain all the benefits they desire from their system.

This book is a simple introduction to programming for users of microcomputers, whether commercial users, domestic hobbyists or teachers. A slight acquaintance with the functions of a computer is assumed, but no advanced mathematical knowledge or familiarity with the detailed electronic construction or workings of microcomputer systems is at all essential for an understanding of the text. No previous knowledge of programming is necessary. The book is essentially a practical guide to programming and a manual of self-instruction. The examples are chosen from familiar fields, and it is intended that these examples and the exercises will be presented to the reader's microcomputer system. Suggested solutions are provided for the exercises.

The sections on the Basic language stress the features that form a common core and are found in the great majority of microcomputer implementations. Chapter 7 is devoted to some of the common variations of Basic found in microcomputer configurations. The chapters on assembly language and machine code deal with the features of the four most commonly used microprocessor chips. Since there is a great deal more to programming than the mere coding of language statements, an initial chapter is devoted to pre-coding activities and the final chapter to program development and testing.

I would like to express my thanks to all the manufacturers and suppliers who provided material about their versions of Basic for Chapter 7. I would like also to mention Anne Patricia, whose life was so tragically cut short in October 1978, and whose efforts on Kim 1 gave me the original idea of writing the book, which grew out of our many conversations on microcomputer programming. In a sense, this work is a memorial to her.

I would like to record my deepest gratitude to Kathlyn Bell for her expert typing assistance, to my daughter Julia, who provided an impetus when inspiration flagged, and to the staff of the publishers for their help and guidance.

Peter C. Sanderson

Contents

1

Introduction to computer programming

A computer system that you cannot program has been compared to a tool without a handle. If you have spent many hours in assembling and testing your own kit, or have become the proud possessor of a readymade system, you will sooner or later wish to write your own programs.

A *program* is a series of instructions that enable a computer to perform the task you wish it to do, whether displaying football pool permutations or calculating future loan repayments. It is written in a language intelligible to the computer system. When you write computer programs, you have to be familiar with the particular programming code (or *language*) in which you are working. This has some resemblance to the activities of knitting or map reading, where you have to familiarise yourself with the code in which knitting patterns are expressed or the code of the conventional map symbols and contour colours.

The word 'program' is the first of the many technical terms that will be used in this book. Some element of jargon is unfortunately inevitable in a work about computers. In this chapter unfamiliar terms are italicised when they are introduced, and are then defined. At the end of the book there is an alphabetical glossary of the special terms that you will meet in this book and may encounter elsewhere in your reading about computers.

If you are using your microcomputer system as a student, you will almost certainly need to write your own programs. If you are a hobbyist, you will sooner or later find that the readymade or 'package' programs supplied by the microcomputer system manufacturer or taken from computer magazines will fail to meet your individual needs. Domestic diaries and budgetary systems vary from household to household, so standardised programs are unlikely to meet individual requirements. If you are using a microcomputer system for control of some external device you are not likely to find an exact, tailor-made system to connect to your equipment for synthesising music or controlling central heating or a model railway system. The computer games that you can buy ready-programmed may pall, and sooner or later you may wish to introduce your own variations into them or to design some game of your own invention, for which you will have to compose the necessary programs.

Programming a microcomputer system is essentially the same task as programming a conventional large computer (these are usually called *mainframes*) or the medium-sized computers known as *minicomputers*. Indeed, if you use certain programming languages for your micro-computer, you will find that your programs will be able to run on a conventional mainframe such as an IBM 370/158. Certainly the preparatory work before writing down the statements in the appropriate programming language is common to all types and sizes of computer system.

All computers follow slavishly the instructions in the program. They are not telepathic and cannot tell if you have omitted an instruction because, to the human mind, it seemed too obvious. If you forget to instruct some computers to halt or stop at the end of the program, or forget to ensure that you do not give an instruction to perform division when one of the numbers involved may be zero, you will have a non-sensical answer displayed or printed. When writing computer programs, you have to abandon all human intellectual pretensions and look at instructions at the level of the machine! All instructions in your program will be meticulously obeyed, but the computer will make no attempt to discover whether they are sensible or comprehensive.

Thus programming can be frustrating and demands close attention to detail. Yet it is not insufferably difficult; no more so than learning to play simple tunes from conventional musical notation on a piano or recorder. Highly successful computer programmers have sprung from the most unlikely non-mathematical backgrounds. The rapidly growing number of computer hobbyists shows that there is nothing fundamentally formidable in writing programs and that it can add challenge and exhilaration to your hobby.

The most important rule in designing successful programs is to avoid rushing into writing the actual programming language instructions until a great deal of preparatory work, which will be described in the rest of this chapter, has been done. There is a fundamental distinction between writing the actual instructions (known in the computer world as *coding*) and the real work of program design. Except for the simplest programs, coding is less than a quarter of the work involved. As in decorating a house or a room, the more time spent in preparation, the better, more elegant and longer-lasting is the result. As paintwork on uncleaned or unprimed woodwork soon needs renewal, so hastily coded programs soon need rewriting or drastic alteration. In fact there is a pronounced likelihood that they will not even run.

There are five main steps in preparing a program, prior to entering it on the keyboard or switches of the microcomputer system in the appropriate code or computer language.

1. Ascertain whether the problem is feasible for solution on your microcomputer system.
2. Define the problem precisely.
3. Consider possible methods of solution.
4. Break down the problem into small steps suitable for representation in programming language statements or instructions, and express these in visual form. (This is known as *flowcharting* and· will be defined in greater detail in the course of this chapter.)
5. Document the statements so that it will be easy to operate the program from this documentation, which will also assist when you wish to extend, or make alterations in, the original system.

These steps will be described in detail in the rest of this chapter.

Ascertaining the feasibility of your problem

Most problems are capable of being solved on a computer system if they can be expressed in a logical series of finite steps. In theory, any problem that contains no irrational or intuitive elements can be pro-grammed for solution on a computer, although in some cases the program would be too complex to write in a reasonable amount of time. You can design a program to analyse past form to predict the winner of a football game or a horse race, but you cannot blame either the program or the microcomputer if they fail to select the actual winner, since elements that defy logic are invariably involved in sporting competitions.

Some problems, which in theory can be solved by a computer, will be incapable of being solved on the particular equipment you possess, or can only be solved with a great deal of difficulty. If your system does not have a typewriter keyboard, it is best to avoid applications where you have to enter letters of the alphabet, and of course elaborate graphical displays are not possible if you only have an LED display. If you wish to use a large file of data in your program, it may be very time-consuming and cumbrous to have to change many cassettes of tape during the operation of the program.

You may find you have a program too large for the *store* or *memory* of your equipment. You will easily be able to find out the store size from the manual that accompanies a readymade system, and if you have built your own system you will know exactly how much store you have attached to it. You will soon become adept at estimating the size of a program in the early stages of design. You can then decide whether the problem should be abandoned (or left until more store is purchased) or whether it can be conveniently broken down into a series of smaller problems, so that you can enter results produced by one program into the next program in the sequence.

In the spirit of a fledgeling pianist attempting a Brahms sonata, you may decide that, although a projected program would be feasible, it would be too difficult until you have gained more experience. This difficulty should not cause you to think of yourself as a coward or a slow learner. It has been estimated in the USA that a standard output of correct *machine code* (the most difficult form of computer language, which will be fully explained in the next chapter) for a programmer is ten instructions daily. Therefore you may not be able to spare the time to program a complex problem.

If you are a small business user of microcomputers you will probably also consider the cost savings and potential benefits of introducing a specific microcomputer-based system before embarking upon the programming. Such considerations will also determine which projects are programmed first.

Definition of the problem to be programmed

The easiest problems to define for solution by programming a micro-computer are numerical. There are many published *algorithms* (rules of a procedure for solving a specific problem, often applied to rules expressed in a computer language) for numerical problems, which may need only slight alteration for your microcomputer system. Whether you use these or whether you completely design your own program, you should ensure that:

● care is taken if any number or intermediate result is likely to be zero or negative;
● no number or intermediate result is likely to become too large or small for your system (the processor manual will provide the range of numbers that can be represented);
● you can obtain the accuracy to the number of decimal digits you want;
● you are inserting satisfactory checks on numbers you insert from the keyboard or switches: 'finger-trouble' can easily occur, and is not always easy to detect at the moment when a wrong insertion is made.

If you are programming a problem where you are working with interrupt signals from outside the microcomputer, such as from a model-train layout, you should make sure that in the program definition the precise timing requirements are defined. You will also have to think carefully about what you are going to insert in the program for unusual and error conditions.

Domestic programs need to be as precisely defined as mathematical problems. You must try to visualise the various ways in which your family will enter certain items from the keyboard. If you are working on a calendar or diary application, for instance, you will have to decide whether you will accept 11 June, 11 Je, 11.6 as being equally acceptable entries, and whether you will accept numeric '0' and alphabetic 'O' as being interchangeable. The insertion of checks on keyboard data can be overdone, but it is as well to cater for major variants in the early stages of system design.

In both domestic and business programs you are likely to be involved in the processing of a cassette tape file against information entered from the keyboard. A typical example of this type of application would be the reconciliation of credits and debits that you have entered on cassette tape with entries from a monthly bank statement that are being entered, item by item, from the keyboard. You will have to program for appropriate action to be taken for unmatched items, which will be indicated by reaching the end of the file when there are still items to be entered on the keyboard or by completing the entry of keyboard items before reaching the end of the file. If your expenditure and income entries are on more than one cassette, you will have to program to display a message to insert another cassette. In this type of program you will have to be liberal in displaying or printing messages for the guidance of data entry through the keyboard and for explaining unusual or error conditions to the person operating the microcomputer system. In all programs, you should avoid displaying a result as a string of digits if your microcomputer system can print or display explanatory headings and text with the figures.

Flowcharting

When you have defined the problem, you will have to consider methods for solution and ultimately select one of these methods. You will then have to break the method down gradually into small steps; eventually each step will be equivalent to a single program statement in the language you are using. To a certain extent, the processes of selecting a method and decomposing it into program statements are complementary, since often a detailed examination of a method originally selected will prove its unsuitability. Then it is necessary to start again with the consideration of an alternative method for solving the problem that you have previously defined.

A flowchart has been previously defined as an expression of program steps in a visual form. Invariably you do not leap into writing the detailed program steps, but start with the broad stages in solving the problem. We can therefore extend our definition of a flowchart to include a visual representation of the stages of the process to solve a particular problem on a computer.

The expression of the steps or procedure for solving a problem in visual form is a valuable aid to programming. When a formula is written down, or a series of instructions (like a recipe) is studied, it is difficult to realise that they are an expression of a number of discrete steps that follow one another in time, because we tend to see the formula or instructions as a whole. However, the computer only obeys one instruction at a time, so a flowchart is ideal for the representation of steps in a computer program since it illustrates the flow of steps in time sequence. A flowchart often makes the subsequent steps to an operation in solving a specific problem more obvious and assists in avoiding repetition of steps. It is easier to alter a flowchart than detailed computer language statements in a program, especially for the beginner.

Flowcharts are by no means confined to computer programming. They are used in a growing variety of applications including mechanical assembly, chemical production and fault-finding in machinery. A set of flowcharts for non-computer procedures has been published for general use in British local government.

The shapes of the 'boxes' in which the steps of a flowchart are written have been standardised in BS 4058. Only the two chief symbols will be used in this book, as it is perfectly feasible for an amateur programmer to manage by using only these two. They are:

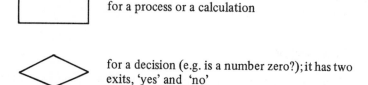

for a process or a calculation

for a decision (e.g. is a number zero?); it has two exits, 'yes' and 'no'

The use of these symbols is shown in a simple flowchart for the game of Snakes and Ladders (Figure 1.1). This example illustrates several important features in the construction of flowcharts:

1. Boxes are provided for 'start' and 'stop'.
2. The amount of detail in a step is entirely up to you. In this diagram, we have included both landing on a 'snake' and landing on a 'ladder' in one box (I).

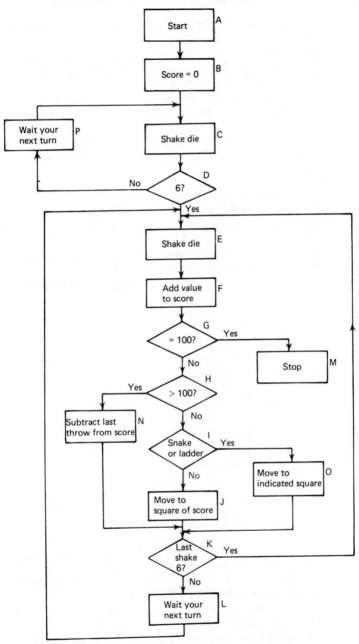

Figure 1.1   Flowchart for Snakes and Ladders

3. There is rarely a single correct solution for a specific flowchart or program. You may doubtless be able to find a different, but equally valid, solution to the snakes and ladders problem. For instance, in box G you could make the test '<100?' and make the 'yes' exit to this the main path of the program.

4. The diagram shows the complexity of a problem that at first sight seems trivial. It also shows the importance of putting the decision-boxes in their correct order so that you can avoid writing identical steps in many different branches of the flowchart or program and (hopefully) avoid any combinations of events where the wrong action is taken.

You may by now be convinced that time spent in planning a program in the flowchart stage will save time and confusion when you are entering the program on the keyboard or switches of your microcomputer system.

Usually you initially flowchart the problem in outline, and then produce successive detailed breakdowns of it until you approach the detailed individual statements of the programming language in which

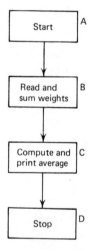

Figure 1.2 Outline flowchart for averaging weights

you are writing. A problem to read-in your monthly weight twelve times and display or print the average over the year is flowcharted in broad outline in Figure 1.2. This represents the way in which humans would solve the problem. When you commence breaking it down into more detailed steps for programming you will get closer to solving the problem as the computer would see the instructions to solve it.

You usually have a method of reference from one level of flowchart to another, so that you can more easily understand the detailed levels —

perhaps some months after the program has been written – by referring back to the broad outline. Often the first-level boxes are A, B, C etc. Then at the second level the boxes referring to A start at A1 and can go up to A9; at the third level they can go from A10 to A99 (A1 expanding to A10–A19, A2 expanding to A20–A29, etc.); at the fourth level from A100 to A999 (A100–A109, A110–A119, etc.) – and so on, as necessary. It is convenient to limit the number of substeps relating to a specific step at the previous level of detail to ten.

The above numbering convention is used in the more detailed breakdown of the weights problem (Figure 1.3). The flowchart has been expanded to include the display of a title and of a message indicating that all weights have been entered. This flowchart introduces the important concept of a *loop*, i.e. a section of program that you want to repeat many times but only write once. All box B of the broad-outline flowchart (boxes B1–B5 of the more detailed one) is the loop here. This type of loop is a very common technique in programming when you know the exact number of items you wish to process. The loop is controlled by a count, which is (usually) set to zero before the loop is entered. When you have come to the end of the processes you wish to perform on an item of the loop, one is added to the count, which is tested against the number of times you wish the loop to be obeyed. If the count is less, the loop is repeated again.

To illustrate the loop in the weights problem, we will reduce the number of weights entered to three (if it works with three it will work with 12, or any number you wish) and observe various totals. This method of checking a flowchart with a very small number of items is a very suitable technique in estimating how correct your program design really is.

Count at B1	Total at B1	Weight entered (kg)	Total at B3	Count at B4	Result of B5 test
0	0	61	61	1	Yes
1	61	63	124	2	Yes
2	124	64	188	3	No

Sometimes the number of times you wish a loop to be obeyed varies each time you run the program, so that you cannot use a count against a fixed number. The usual way of catering for this type of problem is to enter, at the end of the data, a number (called a 'sentinel') that cannot possibly occur in valid entries. An appropriate one for the weight problem would be 0 or –1, which even the most dedicated weight-watcher could hardly hope to achieve. The sentinel technique is very useful and more flexible than using a count against a fixed number. You must, however, ensure that the sentinel value (which

PAGE
44

110

130
140

160

170

180

190

210

230

240

9999

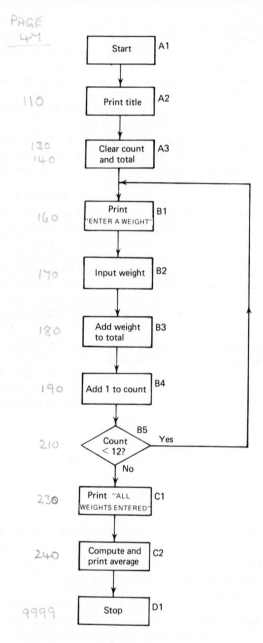

Figure 1.3   More detailed flowchart for averaging 12 weights

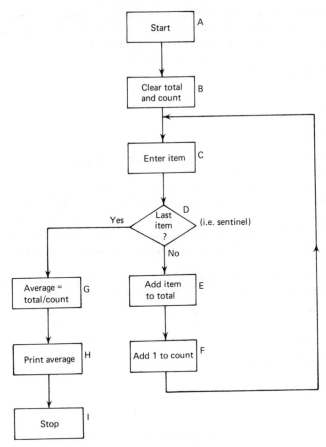

Figure 1.4   Flowchart of 'sentinel' loop technique

could be −1) is tested *before* each data entry is added to the total. Otherwise the sentinel itself would be added to the total.

The flowchart in Figure 1.4 illustrates a solution of the problem to calculate the average of a variable number of items ended by a sentinel. The loop is tested below for data entries of 70, 74 and 0 (sentinel)

Item	Test at D	Total at F	Count after F
70	No	70	1
74	No	144	2
0	Yes		

The previous flowcharts have obliterated each data entry as soon as the next one is read. Often you wish to store each entry for use in a later part of a program. A program to read three items, store each item and (before processing involving each individual item) calculate the average could have some statements of its flowchart as:

Read A
add to total
Read B
add to total
Read C
add to total

The repetitions are obvious here and would be impossible if 1000 items were being processed.

To economise on data-entry instructions and use the loop technique for problems where you wish to save the values of individual data items, use is made of the mathematical concept of an *array*. An array can be considered as a list of individual elements, each of which is identified by the array-name followed by a *subscript* showing its position in the array.

Three weights of 70, 74 and 68 kg can be considered as an array with the name 'weight', the members or elements of which are:

$weight_1$ = 70
$weight_2$ = 74
$weight_3$ = 68

or more algebraically:

W_1 = 70
W_2 = 74
W_3 = 68

The subscript indicating the position of an item in the row or array can be a variable containing a number. If K were given the value 2, the element W_K in the above array would have the value 74. (In some programming languages the first element in an array is assumed to have the subscript value 0, so W_2 in the above list of weights would have the value 68.)

Figure 1.5 is a flowchart for entering 12 weights, computing their average, printing out the average and printing the smallest. Individual weights are saved for some purpose in a later section of the program. In the flowchart K is used for the count, and the smallest weight is stored in S. To ensure that the first weight is, within the loop, stored in S when the loop is obeyed for the first time, a 'dummy weight' of 1 000 000 is initially placed in S. Since, in most arrays, the first weight has to be stored in an element with the subscript 1, the count starts at 1 and at H is tested against 13.

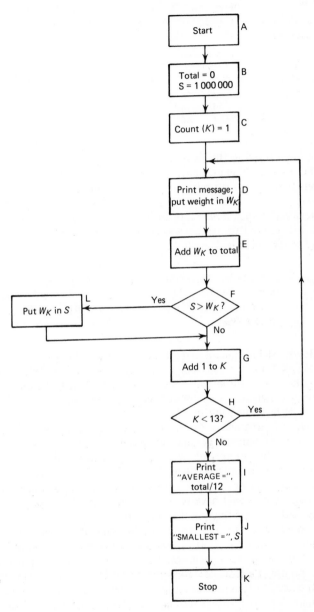

Figure 1.5   Flowchart for printing average and smallest of 12 weights

If the number of weights entered is reduced to three (so that the test at H becomes $K < 4$), certain values during the execution of the loop become:

K at D	S at D	Total at D	W_K	Total at F	Test at F	S at G	K at H	Test at H
1	1 000 000	0	70	70	Yes	70	2	Yes
2	70	70	74	144	No	70	3	Yes
3	70	144	68	212	Yes	68	4	No

The values stored in the three elements of the array W are 70, 74, 68 and the smallest value printed out is 68.

Sometimes you may wish to store items in related pairs. You can conceive them as being stored in a table with rows and columns (or, in mathematical terms, a *matrix*). An item in such a pair (or element of a matrix) is referred to by two subscripts: the first refers to the row, the second to the column. Therefore:

$A_{2,6}$ refers to the sixth column on the second row.

$W_{I,J}$ refers to the *J*th column on the *I*th row; if *I* had the value 3, and *J* the value 5, it would refer to the fifth column on the third row.

The flowchart in Figure 1.6 represents a keyboard entry of 12 weights and heights, for a purpose to be defined in a later section of the program. I gives the row position and J the column position. If the third pair of weights and heights to be entered were 72 and 190 respectively, then $W_{3,1}$ would have the value of 72.

Often in a program or flowchart you find yourself writing the same sequence of statements at different places in the program. You may, for instance, be entering different types of data at various points in a program, wish to process them differently and yet wish to print or display them in a table in the same style or format. Using your current knowledge, you would have to write the appropriate statements of this display routine three times in the program.

Programmers are firm supporters of the principle of minimum effort, and aim to extract the utmost from each instruction or series of instructions. You have already seen how the technique of the loop makes the maximum use of a series of statements. The *subroutine* technique enables you to write an often-used sequence of statements once in a program or flowchart, 'call' it (bring it into operation) as many times as you wish, and always return to the main program's next statement after the subroutine call.

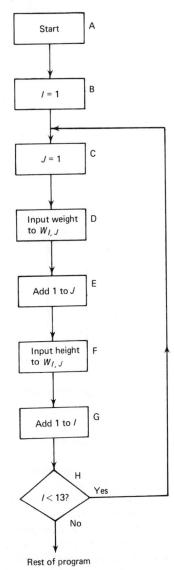

Figure 1.6 Flowchart for entering 12 weights and heights in a matrix

Figure 1.7, which is *not* a true flowchart, illustrates a program in which three different types of data are entered and processed in different ways, but a common subroutine is used for tabular display. The continuous, broken, and thick lines represent the paths followed by the three calls of the subroutine after A, B and C. After each call of

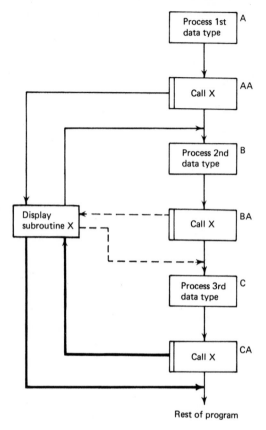

Figure 1.7   Calling, and returning from, a subroutine

subroutine X the sequence of the program continues automatically at the appropriate point.

Figure 1.8 is an actual flowchart that makes use of a subroutine. Two numbers are read from the keyboard, then their average, the average of their squares and the average of their cubes are calculated and printed. The computation and printing is performed by the 'Average' subroutine, which is called three times in C, E and G.

You can write subroutines in one program and then copy them into any other of your programs where their use would be relevant. You can also utilise subroutines supplied by a microcomputer system supplier or written by others than yourself. You must make sure, before you use a subroutine you have not written yourself, that you understand clearly where you should put the data on which the subroutine works,

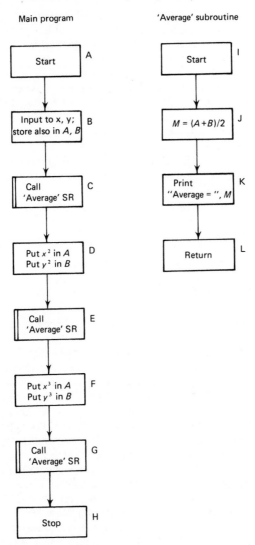

Figure 1.8   Flowchart of main program and subroutine

how the results will be passed back to your program, any limitations on the accuracy of the subroutine, and any error messages it may display.

Subroutines have been supplied for many purposes such as mathematical, statistical, scientific and commercial calculations, graphics and display programming, games, and even for musical output via an audio tape recorder or amplifier and speaker. Even programmable calculators are now supplied with copious libraries of subroutines. In flowcharting, you may find it of assistance to mark the statement calling the subroutine with a double line and to write the statements of the subroutine completely unconnected with the main flowchart.

To conclude this section on flowcharting, it is strongly emphasised that the construction of a flowchart saves much time and effort in the actual coding of the program, and shows many repetitions, errors and false premises. Although there is a school of programming professionals that questions the use of flowcharts in the form described in this chapter, the hobbyist will certainly find them invaluable in showing up flaws in his logic and helping him transform his original ideas into computer language.

Documentation

It is more than likely that you will wish to alter or amend your program after it has been operational for some time. To assist any improvements you may wish to make, it is necessary that there should be some documentation accompanying the program itself, as it is by no means easy after a lapse of time to extract significance from a mass of program coding.

You will not have to provide for yourself or your family the detailed documentation that the professional programmer requires, whose programs often last for years and are often maintained and extended by programmers other than the original author. Yet it will be of invaluable assistance to you to keep the system specification, which described the solution, and the various levels of flowchart you think appropriate for the program. You will find these invaluable in refreshing your thoughts when you come to make alterations or improvements to the original program. You will not have to provide the detailed operating instructions that the professional programmer gives the computer room, but even if you are the only person likely to use the program you should keep an indication of the form in which data should be entered through the keyboard and the action to be taken for error messages. These will provide a helpful stimulation to your memory when you are using a program after a lapse of some months.

The essential documentation you should keep with the program coding is mostly written before you commence the coding itself. The system description or specification and the levels of flowchart are all essential tasks you should perform before the coding. The only additional item necessary for satisfactory documentation is the list of instructions for operating and using the program. These will be written during the testing of the program, so when you are satisfied that your program is working satisfactorily all the necessary documentation will have been previously written. This will be useful not only to other users (whether you are a small commercial user or a hobbyist) but, above all, to yourself whenever you wish to use or change the original system.

2

Choosing a computer programming language

At first sight you may seem to have little opportunity (or even desire) to select the language in which you write your programs. Most packaged microcomputer systems come with Basic, whilst if you are a hobbyist entering program instructions through switches or a hexadecimal keyboard there seems little alternative for you but to use machine code.

However, further familiarity with using the system and wider reading in computer literature, especially the hobbyist magazines, will show you that most systems can be programmed with a variety of languages. Memory addition (which will enable a small system to use assembly language and Basic as well as machine code, and a packaged system to use Fortran or Pascal as well as Basic) is not expensive and the appropriate software to use these languages is available.

You will have to make quite a transition from writing statements on your average type of flowchart to expressing them in a programming language. Computers cannot be programmed in English or any other 'natural' language such as French or Arabic. There are too many different meanings in even the simplest sentence, owing to ambiguities of grammar. For example, 'time flies like an arrow' could have three meanings:

1. Time goes swiftly.
2. A species of fly likes to eat an arrow, on the analogy of 'fruit flies like a banana'.
3. Measure the flightspeed of flies like an arrow would.

Alternative meanings may also be caused by the same combination of letters having different meanings (the origin of the pun and the double-entendre), in such statements as 'Julia has grown another foot this year'. The sheer size of the vocabulary of the natural language, and the fact that there are many synonyms such as:

ADD 1 TO TOTAL
AUGMENT TOTAL BY 1
INCREASE TOTAL BY 1

for the same word or phrase, would also make the use of a natural language for programming very impracticable.

Although many of you will never have cause to use machine code and will skip the next two sections, an understanding of machine code and assembly language will help you to exploit to the full the facilities of your system.

Machine code

All microcomputers have an inbuilt instruction set designed around their hardware. The sets usually differ from one chip to another (although the Zilog Z-80 microprocessor chip will obey programs written in the machine code of the Intel 8080). Even chips from the same supplier have different machine codes as more instructions are added. The Intel 8085 has two more instructions than the Intel 8080, which in turn has 30 more instructions than the Intel 8008, although software written for the Intel 8008 is compatible with the two later microprocessors.

Machine-code instructions are a pattern of 1s and 0s: in other words they consist of *bits* (binary digits) that can only have the value 1 or 0. These bits are entered through the switches on microcomputer systems that are programmed in machine code. Usually if a switch is down it represents 0 and if up, 1. Often the switches on the front panel have corresponding lights, which are on when they represent a 1 bit in an instruction or data item. A typical machine-code instruction, to subtract one from a store in the computer known as the accumulator, is written as:

00001000

On some simple systems (such as KIM) that have a hexadecimal key pad, machine-code instructions are entered in hexadecimal and not pure binary. Each hexadecimal character signifies a group of four binary digits or bits. The numbers 0—15 in decimal, binary and hexadecimal are shown in the table on page 22. The vital thing to remember is that the hexadecimal symbols A—F represent combinations of binary digits, *not* letters for display or printing. These symbols are needed to express the binary groups 1010—1111 using a single character for each (not two, as in decimal).

The binary instruction 00001000, which was mentioned above, could be entered through a hexadecimal keyboard as 08. The use of such a keyboard makes the entry of instructions quicker and more accurate. It must be emphasised that these hexadecimal symbols are translated into binary inside the processor, so it is the binary instruction that is ultimately obeyed.

Decimal	Binary	Hexadecimal
0	0000	0
1	0001	1
2	0010	2
3	0011	3
4	0100	4
5	0101	5
6	0110	6
7	0111	7
8	1000	8
9	1001	9
10	1010	A
11	1011	B
12	1100	C
13	1101	D
14	1110	E
15	1111	F

If your system has only display switches and lights, you will know full well the intricacies of entering the many machine-code instructions needed by even a relatively simple program. Only the hobbyist is really dedicated to machine-code programming. Apart from the considerable length of time it takes to translate a flowchart into the very fundamental instructions and then to key such a program accurately into the system, some other disadvantages are:

● The detailed nature of the instructions; e.g. three instructions are needed to add two numbers and store the result.
● The number of apparently similar instructions for the same process. In the Intel 8080 code there are no less than seven different 'subtract' instructions.
● Complicated methods of *addressing* (reference to the location in the microcomputer memory where a desired item of data is stored).
● The use of numeric addresses, instead of names such as AVERAGE and TOTAL, for data locations. This is confusing and can lead to the use of the same address for two items, with a corresponding overwriting of vital information.
● The fact that different instructions have different lengths, and so occupy varying amounts of space in the memory.
● The total lack of resemblance to any form of mathematical or literary communication.

Nevertheless, even if your system does not normally require it, a knowledge of machine-code programming will often be useful. For example, if you have a packaged microcomputer system that is usually programmed in Basic, you can use the POKE statement (which is often supplied) to insert machine-code commands in hexadecimal to augment a Basic program, and the PEEK statement to examine your insertions.

If you wish to connect your system to various external devices, such as a music synthesiser or an X–Y plotter, you will be forced into writing some machine code. It is also useful in package systems if you are short of memory space, as machine-code programs use less space than Basic statements. A more detailed account of machine code and assembly language is given in Chapters 8 and 9.

Assembly language

One of the earliest potential uses of computers was machine translation language (and one on which relatively small progress has been made in the past 20 years). The concept of substituting one list of characters for another, which is the ultimate basis of language translation, was quickly applied to simplifying programming chores.

An assembly language uses more meaningful representation of the two parts of a typical machine-code instruction: the *operation* code (specifying addition, comparison, etc.) and the *operand*, which states the address of the data upon which the operation is to be performed. A translating program, often known as an *assembler*, performs the translation from the assembly language to the binary instructions that the program actually obeys. Operation codes are usually in mnemonic form such as ADD, SUB.

If you have no typewriter keyboard attached to your microcomputer system, which is essential to working in assembly language, it is still worthwhile to write your program in assembly language and then translate it instruction by instruction as you enter it through the switches or hexadecimal keypad. Although assembly language has many of the defects of machine code (e.g. detailed instructions, inability to transfer to other manufacturers' processors, many almost identical instructions) and should, in practice, only be used when you are forced into it or when you wish to write a very space-saving program, it will produce greater speed and accuracy than machine code.

A common assembly-language statement has three parts:

● a *label*, which is a name you choose for the address in which the instruction is placed;
● the *operation code*, which is of mnemonic form supplied by the manufacturer;
● the *operand*, which specifies the register, address label or literal value of the data on which the operation is to be performed.

Usually these three items are followed by a comment, which describes the purpose of the instruction and may refer to a 'box' of a flowchart. The label field is optional and only used when you wish to reference the location of a particular instruction from another point in the program. For example, if you are going to return to a certain part of a program if the *accumulator* (defined on page 87) is not zero, you could label the instruction to which you wished to return TOTAL (or any other name of your choice); then in the return instruction you would write:

JNZ   TOTAL

Some typical assembly-language instructions are:

START	LDA ITEM	Put an item from an address into the accumulator.
	ADD X	Add an item you call X to the accumulator.
	MOV C, A	Move the contents of the accumulator to register C.
	JMP LOOP	Jump to the label LOOP, and continue sequentially obeying instructions from that point.
	CMP M	Compare the contents of a location you call M with the accumulator.
CLOSE	HLT	Stop (held in an address you call CLOSE).

There are many examples of assembly-language statements in Chapters 8 and 9.

In spite of the fact that it is not really a suitable medium for writing scientific and technical programs or for the processing of business applications, many minicomputer installations use assembly language. Even more surprising is the number of large mainframe commercial and public installations, including one of the largest British local authorities, that still use assembly language as their main method of programming in the interests of economy of computer memory.

High-level languages

Some readers will have resumed their study at this point, as they were advised to omit the two previous sections if they could see no purpose in considering a brief summary of the nature and facilities of machine code and assembly language. Some will have become perturbed at the apparent difficulty that seems inherent, even from a very brief account, in machine-code and assembly-language programming. As mentioned previously, you should try to avoid using these types of computer language unless you really have no alternative or you really enjoy working so close to the hardware of a specific processor.

Most programs in business, commercial, scientific, technical and educational computer installations are written in a high-level language. Most packaged microcomputer configurations for hobbyists also have facilities for using such a language, usually the one called Basic.

A high-level language works in a language familiar to you, rather than in a difficult code that suits the hardware configuration of a specific microcomputer system. As a result, a considerable amount of translation is necessary for a single high-level language statement. If you have Basic on your configuration, try typing in a statement such as:

PRINT $(9 + 56)/(6 + 9 - 2) + 300$

and press RUN, when you will have 305 displayed. If you have studied the previous section on machine code and assembly language you will realise the amount of work the system has done in taking the above statement and translating it, especially in view of the fact that complicated carry flags will have to be set when an arithmetical result is larger than 255 (the largest number that can be held in eight bits: 11111111) and that there is no inbuilt division. Some other possible high-level language statements are:

ADD BONUS TO PAY GIVING GROSS-PAY
IF COUNT = 12 THEN GO TO 100
$a = (c/\log(d - e) + (\text{if } y = z \text{ then } h \text{ else sqrt } (v - z))$

Programs that translate high-level language statements are known as *compilers* or *interpreters*. Compilers were the common form of translation in mainframe computers and minicomputers. A compiler is a program that takes the whole of your high-level language program and translates it as a whole. An interpreter translates each program statement as it is encountered, so in the weight problem in Chapter 1 each statement in the loop would have to be translated 12 times. On a few microcomputer systems you can make a choice between using a Basic interpreter and a Basic compiler. A compiler may take up more memory space than an interpreter, but on the other hand it is not in memory when the program it translates is actually being obeyed.

The bulk of some interpreters must be taken into account if your system has a limited amount of memory, as it will prevent your writing large programs. Another disadvantage is the comparatively slow speed of program execution when each statement has to be translated whenever it is obeyed. The translation or *object program* produced by a compiler is compact, but a compiler is more awkward than an interpreter when you are making small changes to a program, as these involve some element of recompilation. As you found if you tried the PRINT statement above, it is easier to experiment when you are using an interpreter.

Alterations are simple to insert. Most current 'hobby' packaged micro-computer systems provide an interpreter, which is either built into the system or read into the memory from cassette tape.

There are over a thousand computer languages, most of which are obsolete; rarely used; for specialist purposes such as cartoon animation and machine-tool control; or have not been implemented on micro-computers. New languages are constantly being designed, especially in academic institutions, in the endless attempt to ease the problem of communicating with a computer, but most of these are rarely used outside the environment in which they were designed.

Some of the features of an ideal programming language are:

1. Independence of specific computer hardware so that a program is fully *portable*; i.e. it can be run without alteration on a variety of computers including microcomputer systems. This, in practice, is rarely attainable.
2. Rigidly defined so that compiler writers will not make differing interpretations of various features of the language. This helps to promote portability.
3. Is standardised by some national body (usually ANSI, the American National Standards Institution).
4. Uses terms familiar to the user, and is adequate to solve his problems without his having recourse to machine-code or assembly-language insertions to make up for deficiencies in the language itself.
5. The symbols used should be familiar and present on the average keyboard used on most computers.
6. Should be easy to learn and use.

Few, if any, languages conform to all these ideals. It is advisable not to waste too much time in assessing the 'ideal' language for a particular application. All the common ones have their devotees. Below are brief descriptions of the most common high-level computer languages.

Basic

This has the advantage of being implemented on the majority of micro-computer configurations. It was first implemented in 1965 and has been found easy to learn and use — especially by non-professional programmers. There is a great body of programs in this language that can be transferred with some alteration to the average microcomputer system. Each issue of a computer 'hobbyist' magazine invariably contains a Basic program you can adapt for your system.

Its main drawbacks are:

1. Lack of standardisation. There is a *draft* standard for minimal Basic (BSRX3.60,X3J2/76-01) for consideration by the American National Standards Institution, but as of this writing it is still a *proposed* standard. ANSI is also working on a standard for Extended Basic. Currently, however, there is a 'common core' of Basic features, which are described in Chapters 3–6 of this book, to which each supplier has added variations and extra facilities. Chapter 7 consists of a tabular account of some variations in the Basics you will encounter in commonly used microcomputer systems.
2. The 'common core' lacks file-handling facilities, and its output formats and methods of handling large amounts of input are primitive.
3. It cannot usually use names such as PAY and STOCK for data items.

Cobol

This is the most popular language for writing business programs on mainframe computers and is designed for commercial file processing. It allows the user to have mnemonic names for his data, such as TAX and PAY. It has been twice standardised in the ANSI 68 and ANSI 74. Few compilers exist for microcomputer systems. Some of these are *cross-compilers*, where the program has to be compiled first on a minicomputer or mainframe before it can be transferred to the microcomputer system.

Cobol is superior to Basic for commercial processing and there is a great body of professional programmers with expertise in this language. It is unsuitable for mathematical work; writing a technical program in Cobol has been compared to shelling peas in boxing gloves. It is unlikely that you will find a Cobol compiler for a small system. Many small business installations have found they can transcend without great difficulty the limitations of Basic for commercial data processing.

Fortran

This is a mathematical language in which more programs have been written than in any other language. It has been standardised by ANSI, although many programs were written before this standardisation. There are probably more professional Fortran programmers than Basic programmers as the language has been in existence since the 1950s. Its memory requirements for a compiler (you are not likely to find an interpreter) are large, and it was designed primarily for batch-processing of numerical problems rather than 'conversational' use via a typewriter keyboard. You can call variables by your own names, as in Cobol, and the subroutine facilities are greatly superior to Basic, which itself was derived from Fortran.

Pascal

A relatively new language for mathematical work, it has, as yet, not been widely implemented on microcomputers and has not the body of published programs that exist in Fortran. An interpreter may take much memory space. It is rigidly defined but has not been taken over by any institution for standardisation. It combines the mathematical features of Fortran or Basic with the ability to perform file processing. Unfortunately, all names have to be declared before programming, so you cannot just type in

LET A = B/9

as in Basic without declaring whether A and B are whole-number variables, characters, decimal-number variables, matrices etc. There is no operator for exponentiation (raising to a power), but there are functions that some mathematical languages do not possess.

Algol

There are two versions, Algol 60 and Algol 68, both rigidly defined but incompatible with one another. It is an intellectually satisfying language for mathematical problems and favoured in European academic circles, but at the time of writing has not been implemented on microprocessors.

PL/I

An all-purpose language originally designed for IBM computers but subsequently standardised and implemented on other mainframes. It is equally satisfactory for both commercial and mathematical work. The system programming languages PL/M, PL/6800 and PL/Z for the Intel, Motorola and Zilog microprocessors owe something to PL/I.

APL

A comprehensive language with advanced facilities for the processing of both numbers and textual characters. Unfortunately it uses a very unusual character set and is little used on microprocessor systems, though interpreters exist. It is probably the most advanced and comprehensive high-level language. It has matrix facilities and is useful for processing blocks of textual characters.

3

Introduction to Basic

Entry of programs

Basic programs are entered through a keyboard attached to a visual display unit (VDU) or through a teleprinter, so your first task is to become accustomed to the layout of the keyboard. The most common type of keyboard is basically the familiar 'Qwerty' typewriter keyboard with a *complete* set of the numerals 0–9 on the top row. Experienced typists should note that most versions of Basic will *not* accept alphabetic 'l' and 'O' for the numerals one and zero. Some home computers, such as Pet and Sol, have a calculator-like arithmetic key-pad on the left of the alphabetic keyboard. This lessens the chance of confusion in entering numbers.

In addition to the normal typewriter keys there are a variety of special characters. Some of these, such as the Pet graphics, are unique to a specific computer and are fully explained in the manufacturer's manual. Others such as 'Line feed', 'Return' and 'Rubout' (deletes a whole line) are fairly common.

The characters shown on the upper half of a key, for which (as in a typewriter) a depression of the shift-key is needed, should be carefully noted. Much time can be wasted by inadvertently continuing in the wrong shift. One of the most common characters in Basic, '=', is on the upper shift in the most common version of the keyboard. The most common way to delete a wrongly typed character is by depressing the backspace key, as on a typewriter. This is usually marked with a 'back arrow', ←.

If your keyboard is attached to a VDU, you will find it helpful to master as quickly as possible the use of the *cursor*, the small speck of light on the screen, which indicates the position where the next typed character will appear. On the keyboard you will find keys that control the vertical and horizontal movement of the cursor. It does not destroy any character over which it passes. When the cursor is positioned over a character, a new character can be inserted to replace the unwanted one.

Unless you are working in the 'edit mode', a line must be corrected by cursor manipulation before it is entered by hitting the return key.

It is wisest not to have more characters on a line than the line-length stated in your manual, as some versions of Basic would not accept the line.

There are wide variations, in the various versions of Basic, in the treatment of non-significant spaces in a line. The manual for the computer on which you are working, or for the version of Basic you have implemented on a computer you have built, should be consulted on this point. Usually, when a space is allowed or demanded, several can be inserted. This book will indicate the various statements where spaces assume great importance.

You are bound to find you are making mistakes in the initial entry of programs. No program, however, is obeyed until you give the command RUN, so mistakes in the typing of lines will in no way harm the equipment. If you are only familiar with non-electric typewriters you will find the keys very sensitive: the slightest flick of a cuff will often cause a character to be entered, whilst 'double-entry' is quite common for beginners. If you are going to enter long programs or large files of data for the cassette (which have to be processed via the keyboard unless you can invest in a paper-tape or punched-card reader), it is as well to master touch-typing. Eight fingers are invariably more efficient (and after the initial learning frustration more accurate) than one. After you have learned how to program character-strings in Chapter 6, you will be able to write programs to test the accuracy of your typing and design drills to assist the correction of any repeated weakness.

Initially, you can practice entering lines in the 'calculator mode' of Basic, which reduces the computer to the level of a pocket calculator but is useful to gain familiarity with data entry. If you type:

PRINT   11 + 6

and then press the 'Return' key the computer will print:

17

You can use any of the arithmetic signs and familiarise yourself with the * for multiply and the / for divide. You can do more than one calculation on the single line that you are allowed in the calculator mode, so if you type:

PRINT   29 − 10,   6/2

the computer will print:

19   3

(Throughout, the term 'print' will be used for both typed output and output displayed on a VDU.)

System commands

So far you have done nothing with the keyboard that you could not have done with an inexpensive pocket calculator. Before writing programs, however, it is as well to examine some of the commands you give to the computer that are not statements in your program but instructions to the interpreter, compiler or operating system (terms explained in Chapter 2) to perform certain functions with your program. There are variations in these, but some of the most common and standard are:

RUN   NEW   LIST   LOAD   SAVE

(Basic on a terminal to most minicomputers and mainframes has several other system commands such as CATALOG, UNSAVE, RENAME. These are not commonly found in microcomputer implementations of Basic.) The meanings of the above system command statements are as follows.

RUN   This is the most commonly used system command. On some equipment there is a 'RUN' key to obviate typing the word. When this command is entered, the program currently in memory is executed, so this command must not be entered until you are certain that the program you are developing is (as far as you can determine) error-free. When working in the 'calculator mode', where only a single line is executed, the depression of the 'Return' key is equivalent to RUN. If you type RUN a second time after a program has been executed, the same program will be repeated.

NEW   This deletes the current program from memory and allows you to enter a new program. Any values entered in the program that resided in memory before you typed NEW are deleted. With many systems there is a danger that, if you did not type NEW, a new program would be added to the old.

LIST   This lists the current program. It is useful if you have been making many alterations or, on a VDU, where the closing statements of a long program can be moved from the screen, to see the start of the program again.

LOAD   This loads a named program on a cassette or disc into memory. Followed by a program name, e.g.

LOAD   "ANNE'S BUDGET"

it will find that program and load it into memory ready for execution.

SAVE   This writes the current program in memory to cassette or disc. If you wish to retrieve the program by its name, the word SAVE must be followed by the name.

Line numbers

If you are writing a program other than a single line, each statement must have a line number. This is another distinction between program statements and system commands such as LIST: the latter do not have line numbers.

Line numbers start at 1. The upper limit varies with each system. It is probably unwise to have a line number greater than 9999. It is usual to leave at least one space between the line number and the statement, but inadvisable to have a space within the line number itself. For example:

10 PRINT 7*5

would be correct, but

80 0 PRINT 66/3

might cause trouble.

It is usual to leave gaps of 10 between line numbers so that insertions can be made. The last line of a program usually is the statement END, which by convention is often numbered 9999. A very simple Basic program could read:

```
10    PRINT 16/8
20    PRINT .5*6
30    PRINT 3 + 1
40    PRINT 52 − 47
9999 END
```

The complete sequence of commands and statements to run this program would be:

```
NEW
10    PRINT 16/8
20    PRINT .5*6
30    PRINT 3 + 1
40    PRINT 52 − 47
9999 END
RUN
```

This would produce output:

    2
    3
    4
    5

Usually the computer system sorts out lines in order, so the insertion of a new version of a line before END will result in the overwriting of the previous line in the program with the same line number. An omitted line can be typed at any point in the program and will be obeyed in its correct sequence, so the following:

    10   PRINT 8*12.5
    20   PRINT 900/3
    30   PRINT 780 − 380
    15   PRINT 140 + 60
    9999 END

would be obeyed in line-number order, and print:

    100
    200
    300
    400

Remarks

The statement REM introduces a comment that is not compiled or interpreted to produce an instruction. It is useful for program headers and for explaining statements. It can precede blank lines for spacing sections of a program and lines of 'ornament' for embellishing the text, e.g.

    10 REM PROGRAM WRITTEN BY ANNE PATRICIA
    20 REM 19 MAY 1978
    30 REM +++++++++++++++++++
    40 REM IT CASTS HOROSCOPES
    50 REM AND IS CALLED
    60 REM ******************
    70 REM NOSTRADAMUS

For reasons of space, REM will not be greatly used in the examples in this book. Its importance, however, cannot be overstressed, especially if your programs are going to be used by others. If (as the author hopes) you extract profit from your hobby and sell your programs, appropriate annotation will make them more saleable.

The LET statement

10 LET A = 3

The above type of statement is the most common in Basic. It puts the value on the right-hand side of the statement into the part of the computer memory with the name on the left. It enables you to hold computed values, so the following sequence of statements:

20 LET X = 7*5
30 LET D = 19 − 8
40 LET Q = X − D
50 PRINT Q

would print:

24

The names of the 'boxes' of computer memory used to hold information are known as *variables*. The previous contents of the variable on the left-hand side of a LET statement are overwritten by the value of the right-hand side.

The right-hand side of the *assignment* or LET statement can be:

- a number;
- another variable;
- a 'formula' or arithmetic expression, which can consist of variables, numbers, or both.

Below are illustrations of the three types of LET statement:

60 LET V = 10
70 LET P = A
80 LET R = Y/4 − T

In many versions of Basic the word 'LET' can be omitted. If, however, you wish your program to work on most systems, it is advisable to use 'LET'.

Variable names

These are often restricted to the 26 letters of the alphabet or any letter followed by a single digit, i.e. 286 in all. It is as well to mark on your flowchart the use of the variables in a specific program, for example that A contains pay and B contains tax. The REM statement can also be useful in reminding you of the contents of the variables and helping to prevent overwriting of a variable that contains important information.

It is as well to avoid O, S and Z, which (especially when handwritten) can be confused with digits.

Numbers

Numbers or *numeric constants* are used to insert a numeric value in a variable. They can be used either by themselves (as in the 'calculator-mode' examples in an earlier part of this chapter) or in combination with variables, e.g.

    90 LET U = 3.6
    100 LET K = U − 2

There are three ways to enter numbers.

(a) *Integers (whole numbers).* These can be signed or unsigned, so 67 and +67 are equally valid. Commas within a constant are not allowed, e.g. 65,000 would not be accepted. Leading zeros (e.g. 0016) are ignored. Some small versions of Basic only work with integers.

(b) *Decimal numbers.* The whole-number part can be omitted in a decimal fraction. Some valid numbers would be:

    1.96   −11.640   +5.3   0.23   .02877

(c) *Exponent form.* This is only of interest to the mathematician or scientist who wishes to enter very large or very small numbers, which would be clumsy to enter in the forms mentioned above. The exponent form is: argument E exponent (power of 10). Thus 53.7E−2 would represent 0.537. This form of representation is used in scientific pocket calculators.

Each part of the number may be signed. Leading zeros are ignored. The number 567 can therefore be represented in various exponential forms as:

    56.7E+1
    +5.67E2
    .567E03
    567E0
    5670E−1
    0.000000567E9

It is best to avoid typing spaces when inserting a number in E format.

Every computer has a limit to the size of numbers that can be represented (the largest possible number that Pet can hold is 1.70141183E38). An error message will appear if a numeric constant or result of a calculation is out of maximum range. Sometimes, however, when a number is too small and 'underflow' occurs, zero is given as the result and the program continues, as in Pet. The appropriate manual should be consulted about the range of values that can be held. This is not normally a limitation — even the number of atoms in 1.008 gram of hydrogen (606E21) can be held in most microcomputer implementations of Basic.

For readers who deal with relatively large and small numbers, it is as well to examine the precision to which results are given in the microcomputer used. Usually answers are accurate to six or seven significant figures (there is a certain vagueness here, as computers work in binary arithmetic rather than decimal).

Arithmetic operators

You have already met the four arithmetic operators:

   +   —   *   /

There is a fifth:

   ↑   raise to the power of (exponentiate)

This is not as widely used, however, and so is omitted from some of the smaller versions of Basic such as the Tandy Level I Basic and the Computer Workshop 3K and 4K Basic. When raising a number to a whole-number power it is always more efficient to use repeated multiplication. For example:

   110 LET P = A*A*A

is more efficient in running time than:

   110 LET P = A↑3

It has been calculated that a square is evaluated 30 per cent faster and a cube 15 per cent faster, so in one sense you are not losing very much if you are using a version of Basic without ↑.

The expression 0↑0 is evaluated as 1. Zero raised to any other power equals zero. Numbers can be raised to fractional and negative powers using ↑:

   120 LET V = 25↑(1/2)

would put the value of $\sqrt{25}$, i.e. 5, in V.

Combining arithmetic operations (arithmetic expressions)

Variables and numbers can be combined to form expressions such as:

130 LET L = 3*L + 1

At first sight this above expression seems arithmetical nonsense. However, the '=' in a LET statement does *not* signify equality but separates the variable to which the value is to be assigned from the expression that has to be computed to obtain this value. In the above example the old value of L is overwritten. A very common form of Basic statement for increasing counts is:

140 LET K = K + 1

Complex combinations of operations to form expressions are possible, e.g.

150 LET Q = 48 − P↑3 + F $(q = 48 - p^3 + f)$

but these are better avoided if you have any doubts about the way in which Basic evaluates expressions. Some general rules in the formation of arithmetic expressions in Basic are:

1. Operators are never implicit, so 2AB is illegal in Basic and must be written as 2*A*B.
2. A minus sign is treated as a subtraction rather than a negative indicator; for example −4↑2 would be evaluated as $-(4^2)$, i.e. −16, rather than -4^2, i.e. +16.
3. Two signs or operators must not be next to one another, so Y*−3 would be an illegal expression. Brackets are used to overcome this, and the expression could be written as Y*(−3).
4. Brackets can surround any expression. If you must write complex arithmetic expressions, use brackets when in doubt. Redundant brackets are ignored, so long as they are a matched pair. An expression in brackets is treated as a single variable or number, insofar as a bracketed expression cannot be next to another, nor to a variable or number without a sign. For example:

160 LET V = 7(X + Y)   is incorrect
160 LET V = 7* (X + Y) is correct

Brackets help to resolve any ambiguities in the order of expression evaluation: the algebraic expression a^{2d} should be written as A↑(2*D), and not A↑2*D.

Order in which formulae (arithmetic expressions) are calculated

When in doubt about the order of evaluation of an expression, express it in separate statements, each of which could contain simple operations only. Thus you would express the formula for simple interest, $i = prt/100$, in two statements:

170 LET I = P*R*T
180 LET I = I/100

The rules governing the order in which expressions are worked out are given below:

1. When there are no brackets, exponentiations (raising to a power) are done first, then multiplications and divisions, and lastly additions and subtractions. Therefore in the following statement:

    190 LET A = 11 + 2*3↑4

    the value of A would be equivalent to $11 + (2*81) = 173$.
2. If there is more than one arithmetic operator at the same level of working out (e.g. + and −, or * and /), operations are done in order from left to right.
3. When brackets are 'nested' (one set inside the other, as in the following example) the evaluation proceeds from the innermost until the outermost pair are worked out. For example:

    200 LET T = 4 + (3*(2↑(3 + 2) − (6*5)))

    would be worked out in the stages

    T = 4 + (3*(2↑5 − 30))
    T = 4 + (3*2)
    T = 4 + 6 = 10

Brackets can be used to alter the normal order in which signs or arithmetic operators work. As an indication of this facility, each step in the evaluation of the expressions below is worked out so that you can follow the order. (Try them on your own equipment.) A has the value 2, B is 5 and C is 3.

(a) 210 LET Y = A + B*C↑2
                  Y = 2 + 5*9
                  Y = 2 + 45
                  Y = 47

(b) 220 LET Y = ((A + B)*C)↑2
                  Y = (7*3)↑2
                  Y = 21↑2
                  Y = 441

(c) 230 LET Y = (A + B)*C↑2
                  Y = 7*3↑2
                  Y = 7*9
                  Y = 63

(d) 240 LET Y = (A + (B*C))↑2
             Y = (2 + 15)↑2
             Y = 17↑2
             Y = 289

(e) 250 LET Y = (A + B)*(C↑2)
             Y = (2 + 5)*9
             Y = 7*9
             Y = 63

(f) 260 LET Y = A + ((B*C)↑2)
             Y = 2 + (15↑2)
             Y = 2 + 225
             Y = 227

Thus three operators can be combined in six different ways. Always remember, if you find the above and the rules for order of working out arithmetic expressions in Basic complicated, to keep statements simple and allow one operation per statement. Programs are more easily checked and corrected if you do this. The example in line 260 above, for instance, can be more simply written out as:

    270 LET Y = B*C
    280 LET Y = Y↑2
    290 LET Y = A + Y

Spaces can invariably be used at will between the operators, variables and numbers in an arithmetic expression.

Functions

In addition to arithmetic operators, Basic provides some functions to assist your calculations. Many of these are only of interest to mathematicians and are not supplied with the smallest version of Basic supplied with many packaged microcomputers. For instance, of the standard arithmetical functions discussed in this section, Tandy Level I Basic only supplies INT, ABS and RND, while Cromemco 3K Basic only supplies ABS and SGN. Pet, on the other hand, supplies all. The variations in the functions supplied in the versions of Basic you are likely to encounter are given in Chapter 7.

The most useful functions for the non-mathematician are:

ABS   the absolute value of an expression
SGN   the sign of an expression
INT   the greatest whole number less than or equal to an expression

The expression or *argument* of a function is *enclosed in brackets* after the function name, e.g.

    300 LET G = ABS(F + 3.7)

These brackets must be present. The argument can be a variable, a number or any combination of these linked by operators. Bracketed expressions and functions themselves are allowed inside the argument, so some typical statements using functions could be:

    310 LET K = SGN(V)
    320 LET W = ABS(T − (D/A))
    330 LET B = INT(Q + ABS(X − Z))

Functions are evaluated before any operators in arithmetic expressions where they are present. They can be combined in the same LET or PRINT statement with other operators. It is best to avoid typing a space in the function name or between this name and the opening bracket. Spaces, however, may be used inside the argument.

ABS(Y) gives +Y if Y ⩾ 0 and −Y if Y < 0.

SGN(Y) gives +1 if Y > 0, 0 if Y = 0, −1 if Y < 0. Thus, in 'calculator mode', PRINT SGN (−17) would output −1.

INT(Y) gives the greatest whole number less than or equal to the argument. It can provide unexpected results with a negative number unless you have understood that it *never* gives a value greater than the argument; so INT (−2.001) and INT(−2.999) both have the value −3.

If you wish to round a value to the nearest whole number (so that 3.5 would be rounded to 4 and −3.5 to −3) the correct statement for a value held in X could be:

    340 LET R = INT(X + .5)

Using the above statement you can verify on your microcomputer system that the following values of R would be computed from the given values of X.

X	R
11.2	11
17.8	18
−11.2	−11
−17.8	−18
.6	1
.3	0
−.6	−1
−.4	0

If you wish to round to the nearest tenth, a suitable statement could be:

350 LET R = INT(10*X + .5)/10

You will be able to use your equipment to verify that if X was 5.26, R would be 5.3, and if X was 10.78, R would be 10.8.

If you are working with a version of Basic that is not confined to whole-number manipulation (such as the Pet version) you may often wish to obtain a whole-number dividend and a whole-number remainder. To avoid processing the division twice, the following sequence of statements will place the whole-number dividend in W and the whole-number remainder in R when X is divided by Y.

360 LET I = INT(X/Y)
370 LET R = X − (Y*I)

The *mathematical* functions are:

SQRT   This gives the square root. The argument *must* be positive or an error message will result.

SIN   } The argument must be in radians; use the factor of .0174533
COS to convert degrees to radians. To put the cosine of 40 degrees
TAN } in K, the correct statement would be:

380 LET K = COS(40*.0174533)

ATN   The arctangent (the angle whose tangent is) of the argument. This value is given in radians.

EXP   The natural antilogarithm or exponential of the argument. (If you know what this is, you will know how to use it!)

LOG   The natural logarithm of the argument. An error message is produced if the argument is zero or negative. If you wish to find the logarithm to base 10, you must divide the natural logarithm of the argument by the natural logarithm of 10. A statement to compute $\log_{10} 5$ could be:

390 LET L = LOG(5)/LOG(10)

The random function (RND), which is found in most larger versions of Basic, will be described in Chapter 6.

Simple data entry

So far all numbers have been entered in program statements, which has made the programs inflexible. If it was desired to calculate the squares of three different numbers, you would have to write three statements of the form:

    400 LET X = number*number

This is obviously too clumsy for real-life programs.

The READ and DATA statements are used together (one must never appear in a program without the other) and provide a simpler manner of entering numbers than using many LET statements. The following example shows how their use can place the values 11–14 in variables W–Z more economically than using assignment or LET statements. Using LET statements:

    410 LET W = 11
    420 LET X = 12
    430 LET Y = 13
    440 LET Z = 14

Using READ and DATA statements:

    450 DATA 11, 12, 13, 14
    460 READ W, X, Y, Z

The DATA statement provides material for READ statements, *anywhere in the program*. DATA statements need not come before the READ, and can occur at any place before the END statement. The previous example could be rewritten as:

    470 DATA 11
    480 READ W, X
    490 DATA 12, 13
    500 READ Y, Z
    510 DATA 14

It is more usual, however, to have DATA statements for one section of a program before the appropriate READs. Items on a DATA list and variables in a READ statement must be separated by commas. Items in DATA lists may not be expressions.

DATA lists enable you to use the same program many times with different sets of data. Only the DATA statements need be altered.

The READ statement takes as many items as there are variables in the statement from the front of the DATA queue or list. One can imagine the items in all the DATA lists being put into one continuous list and a pointer advanced each time an item is READ into a variable. An error message is printed if you READ more items than there are on the DATA list.

The use of the READ statement does not destroy an item on a DATA list. The statement RESTORE puts the pointer to the start of the list so that all the items can be read again. Thus at the end of the following sequence of statements (which you can try out on your system):

520 DATA −11, 6, 2, 3
530 READ A, B
540 RESTORE
550 READ C, D

you will find the values of the variables, if you print them out, to be:

A = −11
B =   6
C = −11
D =   6

Entry of numbers during program execution

If you are changing the values in which you work each time a program is run, it is better to insert them from the keyboard. The INPUT statement allows you to enter numbers into one or several variables. After execution of the statement

560 INPUT A, P, W

your microcomputer system would halt until you entered the appropriate number of items and pressed the 'Return' key. Often the system prints or displays a question mark or other sign to remind you to input data.

When you have not entered enough data the above 'prompt' sign appears. Most versions of Basic ignore any extra items you insert.

Printing of text

To guide both yourself and other users of your program to make the correct insertions after an INPUT statement, it is as well to print an appropriate message. (Remember that in this book the term 'print' is used both for systems that print on a typewriter and those that display on a VDU.) Any set of symbols enclosed in quotation marks after the statement 'PRINT' will be copied exactly. Spaces *inside* the quotation marks are copied. The statement:

570 PRINT "29 OCTOBER 1978"

would produce:

29 OCTOBER 1978

The following sequence of statements shows a combination of PRINT and INPUT:

    580 PRINT "TYPE TWO NUMBERS"
    590 INPUT C, D

This sequence would remind you, when operating the program, that two numbers had to be inserted.

Simple printing

The PRINT statement above can also print, singly or in a list, variables, numbers and the computed value of expressions. Items in a list are printed in a fixed number of 'fields' on a line if they are separated by commas. The exact number of characters in each of the 'fields' or printing-zones varies; some versions have five of 15 characters; others have four of 15 and one of 12 characters. The number of fields also varies. In a version of Basic that has five print zones, output from the following PRINT statement:

    600 PRINT 5, 3, 5 + 3, 5 − 3, 5*3

would be:

    5   3   8   2   15

The exact positioning of numbers within the print fields varies, but you can soon ascertain this.

Each PRINT statement commences printing in the first print field of a new line. The use of PRINT without anything else in the same statement will leave one blank line.

Text can be combined with variables, and is separated from them by a comma. The following sequence of statements:

    610 DATA 6, 11, 40
    620 READ A, P, W
    630 PRINT "THE PRODUCT = ", A*P*W

would produce:

    THE PRODUCT = 2640

The above uses of the PRINT statement will be adequate for your initial programs. The more elegant alternatives of which the statement is capable are described in Chapter 6.

A complete program

Before attempting to program on your microcomputer system the examples at the end of this chapter, an example of a simple program is given. This is based on the flowchart in Figure 1.2 (page 8). It is a program to input three monthly weights (not 12 as in the original example) and print their average.

```
640  REM PROGRAM TO AVERAGE 3 MONTHLY WEIGHTS
650  PRINT "ENTER 3 WEIGHTS"
660  INPUT X, Y, Z
670  LET A = (X + Y + Z)/3
680  PRINT "THE AVERAGE IS", A
9999 END
RUN
```

Output could be:

```
ENTER 3 WEIGHTS
? 70, 74, 69
THE AVERAGE IS 71
```

Now try the following exercise. Suggested solutions are given at the end of the book.

Exercise 3

1. Input two numbers to X and Y. Interchange these, and print on separate lines their interchanged and original values.
2. Write a program to invert any number between 1 and 99 (i.e. 45 becomes 54; 6 becomes 60). Print the original and inverted values.
3. Using two variables, write a program to print the values of 1017, 43, 1103, 2034, −974.
4. Input a number and print the number, its square and its cube under appropriate headings.
5. Input a number to represent a number of wheels. Print out how many sets of four there are and how many are left over.
6. The monthly repayment of a mortgage loan of £L at P% over N years is given by the formula:

$$\frac{LR(1 + R)^N}{12((1 + R)^N - 1)} \quad \text{where } R = P/100$$

Write a program to calculate this monthly repayment.

The next two problems require some mathematical knowledge.

7. Input two sides of a triangle X, Y and the angle (in degrees) between them, C. Calculate and print the area of the triangle, the other two angles and the third side.
8. Input a number in radians and print it as an angle in degrees, minutes and seconds.

4

Repeating operations in Basic

So far you have only written programs to express the simplest form of flowchart. You have as yet written no programs to code flowcharts with the diamond-shaped decision boxes, where the sequence of a flowchart is interrupted by the test of some condition to see whether the process should continue sequentially or jump out of sequence to perform additional steps, as described on pages 9–11 of Chapter 1.

The problem described in those pages was solved only in its simplest form at the end of Chapter 3. For reasons of space in the INPUT statement, the number of weights was reduced from 12 to three and the program was an expression of Figure 1.2, not Figure 1.3.

From your reading of Chapter 1, you will recall the importance of *loops*, where the same instructions are used many times in a program. Many programs in fact consist of little more than a series of loops. To use this programming technique and program the flowchart in Figure 1.3 you need to use the Basic comparison statement IF–THEN.

The IF–THEN statement

The form of the statement is:

$$\text{IF} \quad \left.\begin{array}{l} \text{number} \\ \text{variable} \\ \text{arithmetic expression} \end{array}\right\} \text{relation} \left\{\begin{array}{l} \text{number} \\ \text{variable} \\ \text{arithmetic expression} \end{array}\right.$$

THEN line number (of the statement to be obeyed if the condition is true)

The value of each side of the comparison is evaluated so that any one of the three possibilities may be compared with another. If the relationship is true, the program obeys the instruction with the line number specified after THEN. If not, it continues sequentially with the next statement. Thus the program branches into two parts. Statements after THEN are obeyed in order.

The operators used for comparing values are:

=	is equal to
$<>$ ($\neq$)	is not equal to
$>$	is greater than
$>=$	is greater than or equal to
$<$	is less than
$<=$	is less than or equal to

You will notice that three symbols differ from conventional mathematical notation and consist of two characters (e.g. $>=$), which should *not* be separated by a space. The correct order of symbols should always be used, e.g. $=>$ must *not* be used in place of $>=$.

The problem of calculating the average weight, flowcharted on page 10, can now be programmed:

```
100  REM PROGRAM TO CALCULATE AVERAGE OF 12
105  REM MONTHLY WEIGHTS
110  PRINT "CALCULATION OF 12 AVERAGE WEIGHTS"          A2
120  REM K IS COUNT, T IS TOTAL, W IS ENTERED WEIGHT
130  LET K = 0
140  LET T = 0                                          A3
150  REM MAIN LOOP
160  PRINT "ENTER A WEIGHT IN KG"          B1
170  INPUT W                               B2
180  LET T = T + W                         B3
190  LET K = K + 1                         B4
200  REM END OF MAIN LOOP
210  IF K < 12 THEN 160                    B5
220  REM BOX C1 IN FLOWCHART
230  PRINT "ALL WEIGHTS ENTERED"           C1
240  PRINT "AVERAGE = ", T/12              C2
9999 END                                   D1
```

This example used just the '$<$' comparison. Some other valid comparisons could be:

```
A = 13
V < > P*Q
N > M + 2
A/3 >= 116
ABS(Z − Y) <= K + G
```

Within an expression the same order of evaluation is used as was described in Chapter 3 (pages 37–39).

Take care in using the '=' comparison symbol

Evaluated quantities may differ by a minute amount, owing to the representation of fractional amounts in the binary form that is used internally in all computers; there may be a minute difference between the values of the expressions 10.5 and 10 500/1000, for instance.

If you are unsure whether statements being compared for equality will be evaluated to whole numbers, the following form should be used. Instead of comparing (X/Y) and Z, when it is not certain that both will have whole-number values, you should compare their difference with a very small quantity, e.g.

$$ABS(X/Y - Z) < 10E-20$$

The small quantity may be chosen with reference to the smallest amount that can be held in a specific microcomputer system. If the difference between the values you wish to compare for equality is so small that you feel it can be neglected and will be due to computer fraction representation (e.g. the difference of 10E−20, which is .00000000000000000001) you can assume the compared quantities are equal. If you have a pocket calculator that can display numbers in 'floating point' (E) form, you can experiment and ascertain that there could be a minute difference between the representation of 10/3 and 60/18.

You may remember from Chapter 3 that function calculation is a relatively time-consuming process. Therefore if you have a function (or any other computed amount with quantities that remain constant each time the loop is obeyed) it is best calculated outside the loop once, stored in a variable and the value of the variable used inside the loop. Instead of writing:

```
250  LET I = 0
260  LET J = 0
270  LET J = J + SQRT(A/B)
280  LET I = I + 1
290  IF I < 500 THEN 270
9999 END
```

write:

```
250  LET L = SQRT(A/B)
260  LET J = 0
270  LET I = 0
280  LET J = J + L
290  LET I = I + 1
300  IF I < 500 THEN 280
9999 END
```

Repeating operations in Basic

The value of SQRT(A/B) is thus worked out only once outside the loop instead of 500 times inside it. You can time these programs on your own microcomputer system, as long as you first insert values in A and B.

The STOP statement

Sometimes, as a result of testing an IF statement, your program may need to cease although the text of the program continues for the other branch of the IF. So far, your 'linear' programs have always ended with the same statement, END, which can be used many times in most systems.

The STOP statement is sometimes used for points in a program, apart from END, where you wish it to stop. It is not usually used in programs that have only one conclusion. STOP is often followed by a message indicating the line where the STOP occurred.

There can be any number of STOP statements in a program. The following example illustrates its use. Two numbers are entered from the keyboard and their relationship to one another is displayed.

```
310  INPUT A, B
320  IF A > B THEN 360
330  IF A = B THEN 380
340  PRINT "LESS"
350  STOP
360  PRINT "GREATER"
370  STOP
380  PRINT "EQUAL"
9999 END
```

The use of STOP immediately before END is harmless but unnecessary.

Important uses of the IF statement

● Counting a number of items for identical processing, as in the weights problem programmed above.
● Ending a process by identifying an input character that marks the end of a series of items.
● Ending a process when the difference between a value in two consecutive executions of the loop is so small as to be negligible.

The second technique was described on page 9. The character terminating a series of input items was referred to as a 'sentinel'. The following program uses the IF statement to recognise this sentinel; it expresses

Figure 1.4, where a series of items, the number of which may vary each time the program is run, is terminated by zero — a character that could not occur in the valid entry of weights.

```
390   REM T IS TOTAL, K IS COUNT, I IS ITEM
400   LET T = 0
410   LET K = 0
420   PRINT "INPUT AN ITEM. INPUT 0 AT END"
430   INPUT I
440   LET T = T + I
450   LET K = K + 1
460   IF I < > 0 THEN 420
470   REM COUNT MUST BE DECREASED BY 1
480   PRINT "AVERAGE IS", T/(K − 1)
9999  END
```

The use of this technique does not strictly follow the flowchart in Figure 1.4, which is literally programmed (with the help of a Basic statement shortly to be described) on page 51. If you use the style of programming above, you must remember that on the last time through the loop the sentinel has been processed (in the above case, since the sentinel was zero it does not matter that it has been added to the total) and that the count is one greater than the number of items. It is a worthwhile precaution, when data is entered from the keyboard, to tell the operator what should be typed after the last item has been entered, as indicated in program line 420.

The third technique is mainly of interest to mathematicians. 'Iterative' techniques are common for the calculation of functions in numerical analysis, and the iteration stops when the difference between the computed value in successive iterations is so small as to be negligible. The following program may be useful if the square root function does not exist in the version of Basic you are using. It calculates the square root (S) of an input number (n) using the formula:

$$S = \tfrac{1}{2}(x + n/x)$$

where x is the previous S (x is given the initial value of 1). The iteration round the loop is continued until the difference between two successive values is less than 10^{-6}.

```
490   PRINT "INPUT A POSITIVE NUMBER"
500   INPUT N
510   LET S = 1
520   REM START OF LOOP
530   LET X = S
540   LET S = (X + N/X)/2
```

```
550  IF ABS (X – S) > 1E–6 THEN 530
560  REM END OF LOOP
570  PRINT "SQUARE ROOT OF", N, "IS", S
9999 END
```

The GO TO statement

So far programs have been obeyed in line-number order, except when the sequence was interrupted by the program following the 'THEN' branch of an IF statement. The statement:

GO TO line number

transfers control *unconditionally* to the line number after GO TO, and the program is obeyed sequentially from that point. (Most versions of Basic accept GOTO either typed as one word or with a space between the words.) The following program, which calculates squares and cubes of an input number and continues until no more input is entered, illustrates a use of this statement.

```
580  PRINT "INPUT A NUMBER"
590  INPUT N
600  PRINT N, N*N, N*N*N
610  GO TO 580
9999 END
```

Control may be transferred either backwards (as in the above example) or forwards by means of a GO TO statement.

The GO TO can be used to program literally the flowchart in Figure 1.4 (for which a version was given earlier, in the example with line numbers 390–480).

```
620  REM T IS TOTAL, K IS COUNT, I IS ITEM
630  LET T = 0
640  LET K = 0
650  PRINT "INPUT AN ITEM. INPUT 0 AT END"
660  INPUT I
670  IF I = 0 THEN 720
680  LET T = T + I
690  LET K = K + 1
700  REM LOOP RETURNS USING GO TO
710  GO TO 650
720  PRINT "AVERAGE IS", T/K
9999 END
```

This is less tortuous than the previous program that solved this problem.

Avoidance of GO TO wherever possible

It is legitimate to use GO TO in the above example. However, a program where control is always switching forwards and backwards, especially if the program is on many pages, is difficult to understand and correct.

You may have met the term 'structured programming' in your reading. In its essence, this technique considers a program as using only three basic types of statement: *sequence* (one statement following another), *conditions* (the IF statement), and *loops* (the IF or the FOR statement, which you will meet soon). With care in choosing the comparison operator and the point in the loop where you make the comparison and increase the count, you can use THEN rather than GO TO.

The program with line numbers 100–240 earlier in the chapter shows how GO TO is avoided by using the comparison $K < 12$ in line 210 instead of $K = 12$, which at first sight may seem more obvious. Below are the rewritten last lines of the program using the '=' comparator:

```
210   IF K = 12 THEN 230
220   GO TO 160
230   PRINT "ALL WEIGHTS ENTERED"
240   PRINT "AVERAGE = ", T/12
9999  END
```

The branches from lines 210 and 220 would cross on the flowchart (an example of what is unkindly called 'spaghetti bowl' programming), and this ending seems clumsy compared with the original. Always think very carefully before you resort to using the GO TO statement.

Sometimes it is not easy to determine the appropriate sequence of statements in each branch of an IF–THEN comparison. This should always be tested with sample data when flowcharting. The position of the count in relation to the test in a loop can alter the sequence in each part of the branch.

Both THEN and GO TO can refer to line numbers both before and after the line on which they appear. It is as well to make sure that they do not refer to a line number that contains a 'non-executable' statement such as DATA or REM. Some versions of Basic will not automatically transfer control to the line after the non-executable statement, and the program will grind to a halt in the same way as when control is transferred to a non-existent line number.

Now try the following exercises, all of which need IF–THEN statements, on your microcomputer system. It is as well to flowchart them first.

Exercise 4

1. Print the numbers 1 to 100 with their squares and cubes.
2. Input 10 numbers and calculate and print their average.
3. Compute and print the reciprocals of the numbers 2 to 100.
4. Using the current rate of exchange, print a table from 5p to £1 and the corresponding values in francs and Deutschmarks.
5. Trains leave A for B and C on the hour and at twenty-minute intervals. They call at B 10 minutes and at C 15 minutes after A. Print a timetable from 13.00 to 16.00.

Try the next problems if you like mathematical exercises.

6. Input 10 pairs of numbers representing the smaller sides of 10 right-angled triangles. Compute the hypotenuse and print all three sides.
7. Evaluate 1000 terms of this series, and print the value of π every 100 terms:

$$\frac{\pi}{4} = 1 - \frac{1}{3} + \frac{1}{5} - \frac{1}{7} + \frac{1}{9} \cdots$$

8. Compute and print the terms of the Fibonacci series:

$$x_{n+1} = x_n = x_{n-1}$$

between 1000 and 1 000 000. The initial terms are 0 1 1 2 3 5 8 . . . .
9. The solution of the simultaneous equations:

$$ax + by + c = 0 \quad \text{and} \quad px + qy + r = 0$$

is given by:

$$x = (br - cq)/(aq - bq)$$
$$y = (pc - ar)/(aq - bq)$$

Input a, b, c, p, q, r and compute and print x and y. Print INDETER-MINATE if $aq - bq = 0$ and NOT INDEPENDENT if $a/p = b/q = c/r$.

5

Loops, lists and subroutines in Basic

All loops with counters can be programmed by the IF statement described in Chapter 4. The FOR statement, to which passing reference has already been made, provides a more economical way of handling loops with counters, as it is designed primarily for this process whereas the IF statement has many other uses (such as testing for input errors) in addition to controlling loops.

The FOR statement helps you by both easing your programming efforts (insofar as you need to write fewer instructions, and have no worries about the relative placing of the count augmentation and test in the loop) and increasing the speed at which your programs run. Tests performed on microcomputer systems show that the use of the FOR statement is between 200 and 2000 per cent faster. A test on two loops obeyed 1000 times shows execution times of 12 seconds using IF and four seconds using FOR.

The FOR statement

Possibly the best introduction to the FOR statement is to code the flowchart in Figure 1.3 using this technique side-by-side with the IF statement method.

```
IF                                          FOR
100  REM AVERAGES 12 WEIGHTS                 100  REM AVERAGES 12 WEIGHTS
110  REM K = COUNT, T = TOTAL                110  REM K = COUNT, T = TOTAL
120  REM W = ENTERED WEIGHT                  120  REM W = ENTERED WEIGHT
130  LET T = 0                               130  LET T = 0
140  LET K = 0                               140  REM MAIN LOOP
150  REM MAIN LOOP                           150  FOR K = 1 TO 12 STEP 1
160  PRINT "ENTER WEIGHT (KG)"               160  PRINT "ENTER WEIGHT (KG)"
170  INPUT W                                 170  INPUT W
180  LET T = T + W                           180  LET T = T + W
190  LET K = K + 1                           190  NEXT K
200  IF K < 12 THEN 160                      200  REM END OF MAIN LOOP
210  REM END OF MAIN LOOP                    210  PRINT "ALL WEIGHTS ENTERED"
220  PRINT "ALL WEIGHTS ENTERED"             220  PRINT "AVERAGE = ", T/12
230  PRINT "AVERAGE = ", T/12                9999 END
9999 END
```

The loop commences with a FOR statement that sets the initial value of the count; each time round, the loop increases this value by the 'STEP' value until the final value (after TO) is reached. The last statement of the loop is followed by the statement NEXT.

The full form of the FOR statement is:

FOR variable = initial value TO final value STEP increment
NEXT variable

The variable after FOR and NEXT (K in the above example) is known as the *controlled variable*. The initial value, final value and increment can be numbers, variables or arithmetic expressions of any complexity. The following are therefore valid:

FOR P = Q*3 TO M/L STEP ABS(R + 9)
FOR A = T TO 8.05 STEP .05
FOR X = −J TO −(Y − F) STEP −7

Every FOR statement must have a corresponding NEXT at the end of the loop. If the STEP is +1 it can be omitted, so line 150 above could be rewritten as:

150   FOR K = 1 TO 12

It is not incorrect, however, to write this STEP in full.

The third example above shows a negative increment. When using a negative increment you must ensure that the final value is less than the initial value, otherwise the program may cycle indefinitely in the FOR loop. This could occur when expressions rather than numbers are used for the initial value, final value or increment.

The following shows what occurs when a loop is executed for the last time if successive additions of the increment do not exactly produce the final value. In the statement:

160   FOR C = V TO F STEP I

the loop would be executed for the last time when:

ABS(C) < = ABS(F)

In the case of a positive loop:

170   FOR K = 2 TO 13 STEP 3

the loop would be executed with K taking the values of 2, 5, 8, 11. In the case of a negative loop:

180   FOR R = −3 TO −9 STEP −4

the loop would be executed with R taking the values of −3, −7.

Owing to the microcomputer representation of non-integer quantities, you should take great care with loops using quantities in the FOR statement that are not whole numbers. In the statement:

190　FOR M = 3 TO 3.004 STEP .001

there is a possibility that successive additions of .001 may result in a value slightly greater than 3.004, with the result that the last cycle would not be performed. The statement is better written as:

200　FOR M = 3 TO 3.0041 STEP .001

which ensures that the last cycle is done. If you have a microcomputer system that is not confined to whole-number working, try this for yourself.

Never assume anything about the value of the controlled variable when you leave a loop for the last time. If you are only going to program one type of microcomputer, the programming manual may tell you what this value will be. There is, however, some variation in the way various systems implement this, so if you are likely to transfer a program to another Basic system it is best to avoid using this variable immediately you have left the loop.

Some problems that may arise in FOR loops

A FOR loop may be executed:

● Never. Some versions of Basic (but not the Pet) skip over the loop if the initial value is greater than the final value and the increment is positive. This avoids the execution of an infinite loop.
● An infinite number of times. This can occur if the computed value of the increment is zero.
● Once. This happens when the final and initial values are identical, which could arise from data insertions.

Usually an initial value (if a variable) can be altered during the execution of a loop, and (if the initial value is an expression) variables within that expression can be modified. As a general rule: **keep FOR statements simple**. Avoid modifying any variable in the increment or final value, and hesitate before altering the variable in the initial value.

An IF or GO TO statement can be used to leave a loop (and not return), to omit statements within a loop, and to jump out of a loop and later return to it. An example of the last facility could be:

210　FOR R = 5 TO 9
220　LET X = R/2
230　IF X < = 3 THEN 370
240　LET T = X/2

```
250   PRINT T
360   NEXT R
370   LET X = X + 1
380   GO TO 250
```

although it would be less clumsy to include the last two statements within the loop. The controlled variable retains the value it had on the jump out of the loop.

You must *never* jump into the middle of a loop that you have not previously left, since you will have bypassed the initial setting of the value of the controlled variable.

Avoid changing the value of the initial variable, step variable or controlled variable during the loop. In some Basics, it would not matter if you altered the values of the first two, as these are transferred to counters before the loop is obeyed for the first time. The value of the controlled variable should *never* be altered. When a loop has been obeyed for the last time, it is unwise to assume anything about the value of the controlled variable after this final exit. You will quickly be able to find out what value this variable has in your own microcomputer system, but you will probably find that it would have another value if you ran the same loop on a different configuration.

All the above precautions may seem rather formidable. In practice, if you use loops in a straightforward way you have no cause for worry. In normal programming you would never feel any need, for instance, to alter the controlled variable in the middle of the loop or to jump out of it.

Nesting of loops

Loops can be 'nested' inside loops. The following program prints the average of five sets of 10 numbers:

```
390   REM START OF OUTER LOOP
400   FOR J = 1 TO 5
410   LET T = 0
420   REM SETS TOTAL TO ZERO
430   REM START OF INNER LOOP
440   FOR N = 1 TO 10
450   PRINT "TYPE A NUMBER"
460   INPUT M
470   LET T = T + M
480   NEXT N
490   LET A = T/10
500   PRINT "SERIES", J, "AVERAGE IS", A
510   NEXT J
9999  END
```

58

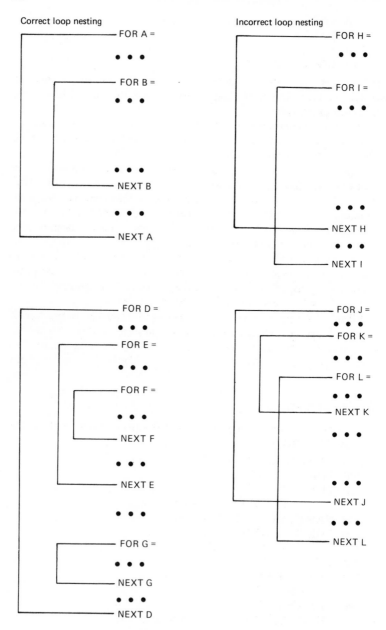

Figure 5.1 Nested loops, correct and incorrect

There is usually some limit (often 10) to the number of loops that can be nested, but you will not find this at all an inhibition. You must never use the same controlled variable in more than one nested loop.

Loops may not be interleaved. Figure 5.1 shows examples of correct and incorrect use of nested loops.

Loop execution speed

You will find yourself using loops a great deal and will wish to ensure that they are obeyed as quickly as possible. To obtain speedy execution, use whole numbers wherever possible for the three variables in the FOR statement. Execution speed of a loop is also increased if you compute as many variable values as possible *once*, outside the loop, rather than inside the loop each time you obey the statement. For example:

```
520   LET Y = 3.141593/180
530   FOR X = 0 TO 85 STEP 5
540   PRINT "TAN", X, "IS", TAN(Y*X)
550   NEXT X
```

is much faster (since Y is worked out once only outside the loop) than:

```
520   FOR X = 0 TO 85 STEP 5
530   LET Y = 3.141593/180
540   PRINT "TAN", X, "IS", TAN(Y*X)
550   NEXT X
```

Exercise 5.1

Now try problems 1–7 on page 53, but using FOR statements this time. Compare their running times with your previous solutions using IF–THEN.

Lists and arrays

You may remember that the idea of an array was introduced in Chapter 1 as a device to avoid input items overwriting one another. An array item, or *subscripted variable*, consisted of an array identifier followed by a number or *subscript* to show its position in the array or list. In Chapter 1 we referred to them as W_1, W_2, W_3, etc., and in the flowchart as W_K.

Many versions of Basic allow a maximum of 26 numerical arrays, with array identifiers consisting of a single letter in the range A–Z. Tandy

Level I Basic, however, confines you to one array only. Some typical Basic array variables could be:

T(4),   X(K),   V(J + 1),   B(H − F)

The subscript may be any arithmetic expression that gives a whole-number answer, although some versions of Basic will ignore any fractional or decimal part of the subscript. It is best to keep your subscripts simple: numbers or a single variable will suffice for most purposes.

The subscript must always be written in brackets to avoid confusion between, for instance, the ordinary variable D5 and the subscripted variable D(5).

Before using an array, you have to declare its size using a DIM (short for dimension) statement. The form of this statement is:

DIM variable name (range), variable name (range) . . .

So a typical DIM statement could be:

560   DIM X(20), V(45)

which would reserve store for an array X with an upper subscript of 20 and an array V with an upper subscript of 45. In some, though not all, versions of Basic there is no need to use a DIM statement for an array when the dimension is 10 or less.

Many versions of Basic assume (like this book) that the first item in an array will have the subscript 1, so the above declaration on program line 560 would have space for 20 items in the array X. Some Basics, however, such as Tandy Basic, assume that the first item in all arrays has the subscript 0. Unless you are desperate for space in your program it is best to assume that all arrays start at 1, even if your system allows a zero subscript, as you can then easily transfer the program to another microcomputer system.

An array should always be declared with a DIM statement before any reference is made to a member of it in a program. It avoids confusion if you do not use the same letters for simple variables and arrays.

The following program is an expression of Figure 1.5 (Chapter 1), where 12 weights are entered and their average and the smallest weight are printed. Weights are stored in the array W, and K is used as the subscript since it is the controlled variable of the loop. Often the controlled variable of a FOR statement is used as an array subscript.

```
570   DIM W(12)
580   REM K IS COUNT, S HOLDS SMALLEST WEIGHT
590   REM T IS TOTAL
600   LET T = 0
610   LET S = 1000000
```

```
620   REM START OF MAIN LOOP
630   FOR K = 1 TO 12
640   PRINT "ENTER A WEIGHT"
650   INPUT W(K)
660   LET T = T + W(K)
670   IF S < = W(K) THEN 690
680   LET S = W(K)
690   NEXT K
700   PRINT "AVERAGE IS", T/12
710   PRINT "SMALLEST WEIGHT IS", S
9999  END
```

The idea of a *matrix* as a table or array with rows and columns was also described in Chapter 1. Some versions of Basic do not allow arrays of more than one dimension; others put no limit on the number of dimensions in an array.

You may remember that a matrix item or element was defined as having *two* subscripts, the first referring to the row and the second to the column. In Basic, matrices may be declared either in the same DIM statement as ordinary arrays or in separate statements. A typical matrix declaration could be:

```
720   DIM A(2, 6), B(4, 5)
```

which declares matrix A with two rows and six columns and matrix B with four rows and five columns. The same letter cannot be used for two arrays of different dimensions. Previous remarks on the use of subscript 0 in some versions of Basic apply equally to arrays with more than one dimension.

The following program reads a matrix with six rows and eight columns and prints the sum of each row:

```
730   DATA (24 numbers)
740   DATA (24 numbers)
750   DIM E(6, 8)
760   REM T IS ROW TOTAL, M COUNTS ROWS,
765   REM N COUNTS COLUMNS
770   FOR M = 1 TO 6
780   LET T = 0
790   FOR N = 1 TO 8
800   READ E(M, N)
810   LET T = T + E(M, N)
820   NEXT N
830   PRINT "ROW", M, "TOTAL IS", T
840   NEXT M
9999  END
```

Now try the following examples, all of which need array variables.

Exercise 5.2

1. Read 10 numbers from a data list. Print their average and the number with the greatest absolute deviation from the average.
2. Divide each item of a table with five rows and five columns by the largest item.
3. Print the largest element of a table with three rows and four columns, and the row and column of that element.
4. Print the prime numbers between three and 100.
5. Print a square of five rows and five columns with each of the rows and columns containing once only each of the numbers one to five (Latin Square).
6. Read from a data list not more than 60 positive numbers, ending with −1. Print the largest, the smallest and the average.

Functions and subroutines

You will have found that the standard functions save you writing complicated sections of program each time you wish to use them; it would be laborious and space-consuming to write your own program lines each time you wished to use TAN and ABS, for example.

Many versions of Basic allow you to use a DEF statement to write your own program line for functions that are not supplied on a specific system, or for processes that you need to use frequently. You are limited to 26 of these *user-defined* functions, and you must be able to express all the functions in a single line. This last limitation inhibits you from complex function declarations (except for the few versions of Basic that allow multiline functions).

The name of the function you define consists of FN followed by a letter: FNA, FNG, FNT could all be valid function names. In the DEF statement the function name is followed by a dummy variable, then '=' followed by the arithmetic expression that the function is to compute. A typical function (to add 15 per cent value-added tax to a price) could be:

```
850   DEF FNV(P) = P + .15*P
```

A function has to be written before it is used. The writing of a DEF statement itself does not automatically perform the function. The function has to be called or invoked in the program when the value you wish replaces the dummy variable. The following short program reads two prices from the keyboard and prints their price plus 15 per cent value-added tax:

```
860  DEF FNV(P) = P + .15*P
870  PRINT "ENTER 1ST PRICE"
880  INPUT X
890  PRINT "PRICE + VAT IS", FNV(X)
900  PRINT "ENTER 2ND PRICE"
910  INPUT Y
920  PRINT "PRICE + VAT IS", FNV(Y)
9999 END
```

You can now see the purpose of the dummy variable, which is replaced by X and Y in lines 890 and 920 respectively. Any arithmetic expression can be put in the brackets (or be the *argument*) when a function is invoked. For example:

FNV(P + D), FNV(P − 20), FNV(P*Q)

could be valid calls of the VAT function.

A version of Basic should (most emphatically) *not* change the value of the variable with the same letter as the dummy variable. Unfortunately, some recent versions do. Ascertain what your own system does, by adding to the VAT program the following lines:

```
855  LET P = 29
930  PRINT P
```

Running the program you will be able to see whether P retains the value of 29. If it does not, you will know that your programs must never use a variable with the same letter as a dummy variable.

A user-defined function can be used in any place where you would use an arithmetic expression, e.g.

```
IF G < FNV(E + Y) THEN 950
FOR J = T TO FNH(E) STEP 6
LET Q = X + ABS(FND(M) + I)
```

Reference may be made to variables other than the dummy during the writing of a function statement. In the following sequence of statements:

```
940  DEF FNQ(J) = A*J + B*J + C
950  DATA 2, 3, 4, 5
960  READ A, B, C, D
970  PRINT FNQ(D)
```

the system should print: (50 + 15 + 4) = 69. Once you use variables other than the dummy in a function DEF statement, however, you make it more difficult to transfer your function to other programs.

You should avoid letting a function invoke itself (the elegant device known to computer science specialists as 'recursion'), as most versions do not cater for this.

Subroutines

The functions you define may be considered as small subroutines, capable of being expressed in a single line, and confined to arithmetical processes. Subroutines were described, in Chapter 1, as the facility to write a commonly used sequence of statements once, use them as many times as you wish at various points in the program, and always be sure of returning to the program statement after the subroutine call.

In Basic a subroutine is a sequence of statements ending with the statement RETURN, and can appear anywhere in the program. A subroutine is invoked by the statement:

GOSUB line number where subroutine starts

To ensure that you do not enter a subroutine except via a GOSUB, it is as well to write all subroutines after the STOP of the main program and just before END. To assist the transfer of your subroutines from one program to another, use high line numbers (this book starts subroutines at 8000) and variable and array names you would not normally utilise.

Below is a program for the flowchart in Figure 1.8 (Chapter 1). Two numbers are read from the keyboard. Their average and the averages of their squares and of their cubes are computed and printed by means of a subroutine.

```
980  PRINT "ENTER TWO NUMBERS"
990  INPUT X, Y
1000 LET A = X
1010 LET B = Y
1020 GOSUB 8000
1030 LET A = X*X
1040 LET B = Y*Y
1050 GOSUB 8000
1060 LET A = A*X
1070 LET B = B*Y
1080 GOSUB 8000
1090 STOP
1100 REM START OF SUBROUTINE
8000 LET M = (A + B)/2
8010 PRINT "AVERAGE = ", M
8020 RETURN
9999 END
```

No reference should be made in a subroutine (by an IF—THEN or GOTO) to a line number outside it, since this will inhibit its transfer to other programs. Any DIM or DEF statement within a subroutine will apply throughout the whole program. A RETURN statement can be used many times inside a subroutine for points at which you wish to leave it for the main program.

A subroutine can call another, although most versions of Basic do not allow a subroutine to call itself. A subroutine can call another written either before or after in the program text. There is usually a limit to this 'nesting of subroutines', but this is not such as to interfere with routine programming.

The following subroutine reads a series of numbers ending with 9999 and prints the number of items, their total and average. It uses another general-purpose subroutine to ensure that division into zero is not attempted (in cases when the subroutine is dealing with mixed negative and positive items such as temperature). It prints a message stating that the tested number is 0 and sets an indicator (Z) to 0.

The main subroutine is entered at 8500. REM statements should always be used in subroutines to show what variable letters they use; when writing the main program you can then avoid these, or see that they contain contents appropriate to the subroutine. Before you start programming it is as well to decide which of your existing subroutines you wish to incorporate, so that there will be no clash of variable letters.

```
8000 LET Z = 1
8010 REM T CONTAINS NUMBER TO BE TESTED,
8015 REM Z IS INDICATOR
8020 REM Z IS ZERO IF NUMBER IS ZERO
8030 IF T <> 0 THEN 8060
8040 LET Z = 0
8050 PRINT "TESTED NUMBER IS ZERO"
8060 RETURN
8500 LET U = 0
8510 REM ARRAY IS Y, TOTAL IS T, NO. OF ITEMS IS U,
8515 REM ITEM IN USE IS Q
8520 LET T = 0
8530 DIM Y(100)
8540 PRINT "ENTER AN ITEM. LAST ITEM IS 9999"
8550 INPUT Q
8560 IF Q = 9999 THEN 8610
8570 LET U = U + 1
8580 LET Y(U) = Q
8590 LET T = T + Y(U)
8600 GO TO 8540
8610 GOSUB 8000
8620 PRINT "NO. OF ITEMS IS", U, "TOTAL IS", T
8630 IF Z = 0 THEN 8650
8640 PRINT "AVERAGE IS", T/U
8650 RETURN
```

Exercise 5.3

1. Write subroutines to:
   (a) convert a quantity in millimetres to metres, centimetres and milli-metres;
   (b) calculate the average of a series of 10 numbers stored in an array;
   (c) apply 2½ per cent discount if a price is over £50 and 5 per cent discount if it is over £100;
   (d) convert pounds sterling to US dollars and cents, at the current rate of exchange.
2. Write a subroutine to print the largest and smallest of an array of numbers.
3. Write a subroutine to print the positive factors of any number less than 100, and use it on an input item in a complete program.

If you are interested in mathematics, try the following.

4. Write a subroutine to solve the general quadratic, $ax^2 + bx + c = 0$, using the formula method, and print the result.
5. Write a subroutine to convert a number in radians to an angle in degrees, minutes and seconds.
6. Write functions to perform the following operations, and use each in a program on three items from a data list. Print the results.
   (a) log to base 10;
   (b) tangent from argument in degrees;
   (c) area of a circle from radius;
   (d) conversion of an angle in degrees to radians;
   (e) rounding of a positive number, e.g. 1.5 becomes 2;
   (f) cube root.

6

Some additional Basic facilities

The facilities discussed so far are generally common to most versions of Basic — even the 'tiny Basics' that use very little memory. (Some of the omissions of certain variants are listed in Chapter 7.) This chapter describes some features that are less common but are found in many microcomputer versions and will be familiar to readers who have used Basic on minicomputers and mainframes. Since these facilities are less usual, there is a correspondingly greater variation in the manner in which they are implemented.

Character handling

So far you have only worked with numbers. Your only contact with non-numerical data items has been with the PRINT " " statement, which enabled you to print messages and titles. You have not been able to read characters from the keyboard or from data lists, and have not been able to compare or sort characters. These facilities are of growing importance, in view of the increase in text processing and word processing in business and the increase in the amount of character information (such as recipes and address lists) that most home computer users wish to store and use.

Characters in Basic are considered as being held in a *string*, which is a sequence of characters treated as a unit. You have already met this in the PRINT statement, where the characters inside the quotation marks are a string. An element of a string can be any character (including a space) of the character set in the microcomputer configuration you are using.

Character strings are held in *string variables*, which are denoted by a letter followed by a $ sign. The size of the string that can be held in a single variable varies considerably (from 15 to 4096 in some current versions of Basic). Your programming manual for the computer you are using will guide you on this. If you wish to be able to use your programs on computer configurations other than your own it is as well not to let your strings exceed the maximum of 15 characters. Some small versions of Basic do not allow string variables, or else they allow you to have just one. Some versions of Basic permit string arrays: A$(1) would refer to the first member of string array A$. (There is no relation between a *numerical* variable or array and a *string* variable or array with the same letter, so whatever you do to W will not alter the contents of the string variable W$.)

Some versions of Basic allow a 'null string', which contains no characters and can be set by the LET command:

```
100   LET R$ = " "
```

This is usually used to clear the space used by a lengthy string, in versions of Basic that allow the storage of long character strings in a single variable.

Character values (which can be a single character) can be inserted in character variables by a LET statement (as above), a DATA statement (in which numerical and character data can be mixed, provided they are separated by commas) or an INPUT statement:

```
110   LET T$ = "PARADISE"
120   DATA 5, "LOST", 7, "BY JOHN MILTON"
130   READ U, V$, X, Y$
140   INPUT Z$
```

In the above examples, T$ would contain PARADISE and V$ LOST and Y$ BY JOHN MILTON and Z$ whatever was entered from the keyboard. As in the PRINT statement, spaces are important in a string; they are counted in the number of characters and held in storage (as in Y$ above).

String variables cannot be used to hold numbers for arithmetical calculation, so the statement:

```
150   LET G = J$ + B$
```

would be illegal (just as numerical variables cannot be used to hold characters). A string can of course contain numbers or symbols not used arithmetically, e.g.

```
160   LET F$ = "JANUARY 1980"
170   LET H$ = "*_*_*"
```

Characters can be output from strings by the PRINT statement, as in the following sequence of statements:

```
180   LET Q$ = "LORNA"
190   LET J$ = "OXLEY"
200   PRINT Q$, J$
```

which would print or display:

    LORNA   OXLEY

As in the READ statement, the PRINT statement can hold mixed numerical and character data; for example, the sequence of statements:

```
210  DATA 11, 6, "ANNE"
220  READ A, B, C$
230  PRINT A, B, "1940", C$, "PATRICIA"
```

would print:

    11   6   1940   ANNE   PATRICIA

You cannot do any really useful work with character information unless the computer can sort it in order and identify a string (as in the case where you type YES or NO in answer to a query on the display). To make such comparisons possible, characters are given an order of value, or *collation sequence*, which will vary according to the particular microcomputer configuration you are using. In any scheme $A < Z$ and $0 < 9$, and space is usually regarded as the smallest character, but there are differences in the ranking of symbols and punctuation marks. The following sequence of statements shows a simple string comparison:

```
240  PRINT "DO YOU WISH TO CONTINUE"
250  PRINT "TYPE YES OR NO"
260  INPUT L$
270  IF L$ = "NO" THEN 9999
     (rest of program)
```

If two strings of different lengths are being compared, the whole of the shorter string and the corresponding part of the other are used. If the string and part-string are then found to be equal, the shorter string is considered the smaller. Thus in the following sequence of statements, 2 is printed:

```
280  DATA "ANNE, "ANN"
290  READ V$, G$
300  IF V$ > G$ THEN 330
310  PRINT "1"
320  STOP
330  PRINT "2"
```

You will have to check the value of a space in the collating sequence if you are using letter-by-letter rather than word-by-word sorting technique, so that you will know whether "ABBEY WOOD" is counted greater or less than "ABBEYFIELD".

Some versions of Basic have string functions such as LEN(Z$), which would give the number of characters held in the variable Z$. These are not discussed here, as there is wide variation in their facilities in the various implementations of Basic.

Further printing facilities

The various options of the PRINT statement differ widely in the various implementations of Basic. The features discussed in this section are, however, common to most.

If you wish to leave a blank line on the paper or your VDU, the use of PRINT alone in a statement will perform this facility. The following series of statements:

```
340   DATA 11, 5, 62
350   READ A, B, C
360   PRINT "JULIA'S BIRTHDAY IS"
370   PRINT
380   PRINT A, B, C
```

would produce the output:

JULIA'S BIRTHDAY IS

11   5   62

So far your output has been restricted by the print zones (as in the above example where the three numbers are widely separated). Most versions of Basic have different zone widths: one version has five columns of 15 character positions. However, the print zones can be overridden if you separate items by a semicolon instead of a comma. In this way you can print more information on a single line. The number of spaces between each item using the semicolon separator varies. One version inserts two spaces if the items are numeric, one space if one item is numeric and the other a character string, and no spaces where both items are strings.

Experiment on your own microcomputer configuration will quickly show you the exact spacing used in both the semicolon and comma modes of separating print items. If the PRINT statement in either mode contains more items than can be printed on a single line, the printing will automatically continue on the next line.

The contrast between the semicolon and comma modes is shown in the following statements:

```
390   DATA 6, 60, 600, 6000, 60000
400   READ V, W, X, Y, Z
```

```
410  PRINT V, W, X, Y, Z
420  PRINT V; W; X; Y; Z
430  PRINT "THIS", "IS", "AN", "EXAMPLE"
440  PRINT "THIS"; "IS"; "AN"; "EXAMPLE"
```

which would produce:

```
6       60      600      6000     60000
6  60  600  6000  60000
THIS        IS        AN        EXAMPLE
THISISANEXAMPLE
```

If you wish to print out numbers containing decimal fractions it is more appropriate to use the comma mode of printing, in which the points are automatically aligned under each other.

If you end a PRINT statement with a comma or semicolon the printing is automatically (if there is room) continued on the same line, as the following example shows:

```
450  DATA 1, 2, 3, 4
460  READ A, B, C, D
470  PRINT A, B,
480  PRINT C, D
490  PRINT A; B;
500  PRINT C; D
```

which would produce output as:

```
1       2       3       4
1  2  3  4
```

Semicolon and comma modes may be mixed in the same PRINT statement. If the above sequence of statements continued:

```
505  PRINT "RESULTS ARE"; A, B, C
```

the output would be:

```
RESULTS ARE 1       2       3
```

The TAB function is common to most versions of Basic. The form is:

TAB(whole-number expression)

The whole-number expression represents the character position, counting from the left-hand margin. If the above sequence of statements continued:

```
505 PRINT TAB(8); A; TAB(20); B
```

output would be produced as:

```
       1            2
```

The TAB function is overridden by the comma and semicolon formats, so you must be sure that the argument is greater than the number of spaces that your version of Basic would normally provide with these formats. You can use TAB to align items if you are using the semicolon mode, and to print rough graphs on a printer or typewriter if you have no VDU or graphics symbols.

Files

Most versions of Basic have file facilities: these enable you to read and write to and from magnetic disc or cassette tape, so that you can use information previously created. Disc statements vary widely, so this section will concentrate on cassette-type files. You may have already met these for saving programs, where you use the instruction SAVE.

Before you use a file of data or information in Basic the file must be 'opened', even if you are going to write a new file on a virgin tape. One form of the OPEN statement is:

OPEN logical file number, physical device number, input/output option, file-name

You provide a *logical file number* in the program, and you use this number when reading or writing to this file. There is usually a limit on the number of logical files that can be used in a single program.

The *physical device number* (e.g. cassette drive number if you are using a system that has more than one) will be specified in the manual for the configuration you use.

The *input/output option* defines whether you wish to read a file (and inhibit any future user of the program from writing on it), write it, or both read and write it. These options can control the setting of end-of-tape and end-of-file markers.

There is usually a limit on the number of characters you can use in a *file-name*. It is as well to ensure that the opening letters of two files are not identical, as a search for the shorter name of the two may not always provide the correct file.

At the end of a program each file must be closed. The appropriate statement is:

CLOSE logical file number

Depending upon the option used in the corresponding OPEN statement, end-of-file and end-of-tape markers are written. No work can be done on a file after it has been closed, so care should be taken to ensure that a CLOSE statement does not occur in a loop that you wish to obey several times. If you omit to close a file, it may become garbled.

Files are read by the INPUT statement, the form of which for reading a file is:

INPUT# logical file number, variables

(The 'hash' sign # is replaced by a colon in some Basics.) A short program to read the first three items of a file and print them could be:

```
510  OPEN 1, 1, 0, JANSTATS
520  INPUT# 1, A, B, C
530  PRINT "START OF FILE IS"; A, B, C
540  CLOSE 1
```

If your version of Basic allows you to use INPUT (and not GET) for character information from a file, you must ensure that you have a character variable in the appropriate place after INPUT.

Files are written using a form of the PRINT statement; in many versions PRINT is followed by # logical file number. There is often some limitation on the number of items (in PET it is 80) that you can write to a file at any one time without a carriage return. The following sequence of statements shows a title and 80 items of data written to a file:

```
550  OPEN 1, 1, 2, DECSTATS
560  PRINT# 1, "DECEMBER 1979 SALES"
570  PRINT "ENTER 80 ITEMS"
580  FOR J = 1 TO 80
590  INPUT A
600  PRINT# 1, A
610  NEXT J
620  CLOSE 1
```

Of necessity, this section on file processing has been of a general nature as details vary greatly in the various versions of Basic. Programs that contain file statements are rarely completely transferable from one microcomputer to another.

The RND function

Most versions of Basic include the RND function for the generation of random numbers. These are useful if you are writing programs to simulate games of chance, or writing a model of some situation where random events occur. In practice the numbers generated are pseudo-random. Truly random numbers would make a cycle of numbers almost impossible to repeat, which would make an identical repetition of an experiment unattainable and would produce difficulties in testing and debugging programs.

The classic form of the random-number function is:

RND(X)

where X is a whole-number argument. Thus a statement of the form:

630   LET R = RND(1)

would produce a random positive fraction between 0 and 1.
On one system the following sequence of statements:

640   FOR K = 1 TO 3
650   PRINT RND(1)
660   NEXT K

would produce output:

.2435041   .2998482   .6075527

Numbers produced are usually unique to a specific system.

Unfortunately, in various versions of Basic there is a great variety in the argument (if any) after RND, and in the numbers produced. In Pet, a negative argument starts a new series of random numbers; a zero argument gives the last random number generated, while an argument greater than zero will generate a new random number between 0 and 1.

Some systems require no argument, while NIBL (National Industrial Basic Language) uses two arguments and returns a whole number between them. In this book the argument 1 will always be used, and it will be assumed that a positive decimal fraction is produced. The manual for the system you are using will give details of how variations in the argument produce differing results and how you can repeat a desired sequence of pseudo-random numbers.

One method of varying the sequence is to type in a variable each time the program is run, to indicate how many successive pseudo-random numbers are to be ignored before they are used:

670   PRINT "TYPE HOW MANY RANDOMS TO BE IGNORED"
680   INPUT K
690   FOR J = 1 TO K
700   LET Y = RND(1)
710   NEXT J

If the sequence previously quoted (640–660) were used with the above statements and '2' were entered at the keyboard, the first random number you would obtain after leaving the above loop would be .6075527.

If your RND function gives you a fraction it can be converted to an integer by multiplying by an appropriate power of 10. The sequence of statements:

```
720  FOR K = 1 TO 50
730  PRINT 100*RND(1)
740  NEXT K
```

would produce 50 random numbers in the range 0–100.

If you wish to simulate tossing a coin, the following statement will give either 0 or 1 (heads or tails) with a probability of .5:

```
750  LET C = INT(RND(1) + .5)
```

If you wish to imitate the casting of an unbiased die, where six results are equally probable, the program statement would be:

```
760  LET D = INT(6*RND(1)) + 1
```

Other facilities

Most of the facilities discussed in this chapter are implemented with a great deal of variety and difference in various versions of Basic. There are many other facilities that some versions of Basic for microcomputer systems possess, such as:

- matrix functions;
- character string functions;
- PEEK and POKE statements for machine-code working;
- graphics facilities;
- cursor-control statements.

These are not as common as the features discussed in this chapter, however.

Now try the following exercise.

Exercise 6

1. Read five words from a data list, sort them and print them in alphabetical order.
2. Input a number, and print in a word the remainder when it is divided by 11.
3. Read 10 whole numbers smaller than 30, and beside each print a bar chart (using +s) showing the value of each number, e.g.

   5   +++++

4. Simulate 100 throws of a dice, and print the number of times each face appears.
5. Simulate the dealing of 13 cards from a single pack, and print the hand.
6. A roulette wheel is numbered 0–36 (ignore 0). Simulate 1000 spins of the wheel, and print out the number of times you find Pair (even), Impair (odd), Manque (1–18) and Passe (19–36).

7

Variants of Basic

Basic has never been defined with the rigour of Cobol or Fortran. Reference has been made in Chapters 3–6 to the availability of certain features such as the ability to process character strings by function and the number of permitted arrays. Most suppliers of Basic compilers or interpreters have added features if they were using a reasonable amount of memory space for the translating software, so there are numerous 'extended Basics', most of which contain some unique features. On the other hand, the versions of Basic that operate in very small amounts of memory (the 'tiny Basics') omit certain standard features, such as the ability to manipulate numbers with a decimal part. Some variations in Basic arise from the number of bytes used to hold numbers and the way in which decimal fractions are represented.

The table in this chapter contains information about some versions of Basic that you may encounter in packaged microcomputer systems. This should act as a guide if you are choosing a system and it is vital that it can cope with some features such as the processing of numbers with a decimal part. The versions described have been in use for some time, so it is not likely that their essential facilities will radically change.

Chapters 3–6 contained information about what may be defined as the 'common core' of microcomputer implementations of Basic. Many additions to this have been made, such as:

- the ability to omit LET in an assignment statement;
- multiple statements on a single line;
- character functions;
- use of AND and OR in an IF statement;
- commands for graphics.

The reference in the table to 'all functions' means that the version contains the functions:

RND, ABS, SGN, INT, SIN, COS, TAN, ATN, LOG, EXP, SQR

The reference to 'all arithmetic operators' means the inclusion of:

$\uparrow$ + $-$ * /

The reference to 'all relational operators' means the inclusion of:

= <> >= > <= <

	Altair/MITS: Disk Extended	Apple Integer	Applesoft
1. Integer only	No	Yes	No
2. Character variables	Yes	Yes	Yes
3. Character functions	Yes	Yes	Yes
4. All functions	Yes	Only RND, SGN, ABS	Yes
5. All arithmetic operators	Yes	Yes	Yes
6. All relational operators	Yes	Yes	Yes
7. Matrix instructions	No	No	No
8. User-defined functions	Yes	Yes	Yes
9. Multi- dimensional arrays	Yes	No	Yes
10. Graphics facilities	No	Yes	Yes
11. PEEK and POKE	Yes	Yes	Yes
12. Maximum number held	32 767	32 767	
13. File-handling facilities	Yes		Yes
14. Some additional facilities/ restrictions	Versatile print formats. Diagnostics. Disc data files.	Colour graphics. No READ, DATA. Diagnostics. Program chaining.	Colour graphics. Incompatible with INTEGER. Logical operators.

	Crofton Electronics: NIBL	Crofton Electronics: 8K disc interactive Basic	Cromemco: Control Basic
1. Integer only	Yes	No	Yes
2. Character variables	Yes	Yes	Yes
3. Character functions	No	Yes	
4. All functions	RND, MOD the only arithmetical ones	Yes	SGN, ABS, RND
5. All arithmetic operators	No ↑	Yes	No ↑
6. All relational operators	Yes	Yes	Yes
7. Matrix instructions	No	No	No
8. User-defined functions	No	No	No
9. Multi-dimensional arrays	No arrays	Two only	None
10. Graphics facilities	No	No	No
11. PEEK and POKE	Indirect operator does this function	Yes	No
12. Maximum number held	32 767	9.999E+99	32 767
13. File-handling facilities	No	Yes	No
14. Some additional facilities/ restrictions	A 'tiny Basic'. Allows multiple statements on a line.	Interactive data files. Editing facilities. Diagnostic aids.	Occupies 3K. Can call machine-code subroutines.

Cromemco: 16K Basic	Computer Software Services: Super Basic	CW 6800: 3K Basic	CW 6800: 8K Basic
No	No	Yes	No
Yes	Yes	No	Yes
Yes	Yes	No	Yes
Yes	Yes	ABS, INT, RND, SGN	No ATN
Yes	Yes	No ↑	Yes
Yes	Yes	Yes	Yes
No	No	No	No
Yes	Yes	No	Yes
3 dimensions	2 dimensions	No	Yes
No	Yes	No	No
Yes	Yes	No	Yes
9.99E+62	9.99E+99	32 767	
Yes	Yes	No	No
8 files can be open at any one time. Programs can be chained. Diagnostics.	Commands can be abbreviated. Programs can be chained.	No READ, DATA.	Peripheral handling. Dis-assembler.

	Midas M100 Basic	MVT Basic (Altair)	North Star Extended Basic 5-PFB
1. Integer only	No	No	No
2. Character variables	Yes	Yes	Yes
3. Character functions	Yes	Yes	Yes
4. All functions	Yes	No EXP	Yes
5. All arithmetic operators	Yes	Yes	Yes
6. All relational operators	Yes	Yes	Yes
7. Matrix instructions	No	No	No
8. User-defined functions	Yes	Yes	Yes
9. Multi-dimensional arrays	Yes	Yes	Yes
10. Graphics facilities	Yes	No	No
11. PEEK and POKE	Yes	No	Yes
12. Maximum number held	9E+18		14-digit precision
13. File-handling facilities	Yes	Yes	(Inversion 6)
14. Some additional facilities/ restrictions	Character editor. Multiple statements on a line. Diagnostics. Disc-file processing.	Compiler and re-entrant run time package. Diagnostics. Random-access files.	Multiple line user function definitions. Logical operators. Program renumber capability.

Pet	Research machines: Tiny Basic interpreter	Research machines: 9K Basic	Research machines: 12K Basic
No	Yes	No	No
Yes	No	Yes	Yes
Yes	No	Yes	Yes
Yes	ABS, RND	Yes	Yes
Yes	No	Yes	Yes
Yes	Yes	Yes	Yes
No	No	No	No
Yes	No	Yes	Yes
Yes	No	Yes	Yes
Yes	Yes	Yes	Yes
Yes	No	Yes	Yes
1.701411838E+38	32 767	1E+38	1E+38
Yes	No	Yes	Yes
Graphics keyboard. Multiple statements on a line. Diagnostics. Screen edit facility.	Multiple statements on a line. Abbreviated commands. Expressions can be substituted for values.	On-line editing. Diagnostics. Two independent output streams.	As 9K Basic, plus: Automatic generation of line numbers. Multiline functions.

82

	SOL: Basic 5	SOL: Extended Cassette Basic	Sorcerer Standard Basic
1. Integer only	No	No	No
2. Character variables		Yes	Yes
3. Character functions	No	Yes	Yes
4. All functions	No ATN	Yes	Yes
5. All arithmetic operators	Yes	Yes	Yes
6. All relational operators	Yes	Yes	Yes
7. Matrix instructions	No	Yes	No
8. User-defined functions	No	Yes	Yes
9. Multi-dimensional arrays	No	Yes	Yes
10. Graphics facilities	No	Yes	Yes
11. PEEK and POKE	No	Yes	Yes
12. Maximum number held	.9999E+127	.9999E+127	
13. File-handling facilities	Yes	Yes	No
14. Some additional facilities/ restrictions	Editing. 6 nested subroutines.	Diagnostics. Some parts of compiler can be taken from memory. Automatic renumbering. Logical operators.	User-defined graphic symbols. Upper and lower case alphanumerics.

Tandy TRS80 Level I Basic	Tandy TRS80 Level II Basic
Yes	No
Two	Yes
No	Yes
ABS, RND	Yes
No ↑	Yes
Only = > <	Yes
No	No
No	Yes
No	Yes
Yes	Yes
No	Yes
1E+38	1.701411E+38
No	Yes
Only 1 array allowed. Abbreviated command words.	Incompatible with level I. Double-precision variables available. 900 variable names. 5 types of variable.

8

Introduction to assembly-language and machine-code programming

This chapter is an introduction to the useful features of assembly-language and machine-code programming, rather than a detailed guide to the programming of a specific microprocessor. It describes some aspects that will be of assistance, but does not deal at great length with some of the more intricate facilities of specific chips.

If you are using a packaged microcomputer system for business, ordinary domestic, or scientific calculation work then it is unlikely that you will prefer this type of language to Basic. If, however, you wish to link your system to an external control device or to some non-standard peripheral, such as an analogue-to-digital converter or an amplifier, you will have to write the appropriate software interface in assembly language or machine code. The provision of PEEK and POKE statements in most versions of Basic on packaged systems appears to indicate some awareness of the need to use machine code on occasions.

Undoubtedly machine-code programs are a great deal faster than high-level language ones, but this execution speed must be balanced against the time occupied by their writing and development, and by the fact that a Basic program with machine-code insertions is not transferable to systems based on a different microprocessor. However, there is nothing inherently difficult about programming in a low-level language. Until the early 1960s, when Fortran was fully developed, most technical programs were written in assembly language. This language was also very widely used for the programming of business applications until the late 1960s, and thousands of programmers were trained in it. So do not be put off — assembly-language and machine-code programming is by no means as difficult as it may first appear.

You may find it useful to read pages 21–24 of Chapter 2 again, to refresh your memory of some of the terminology. This will also remind you of the binary and hexadecimal systems. Examples in this chapter will be written in assembly language, from which you can derive the machine code by referring to the operation code on the code card of the system you are using and, where appropriate, attaching an address of your choice.

For instance, using the Intel 8080 code, if you were working on a payroll program and wished to store the computed pay in address 260, your translation would appear as:

```
STA PAY     00110010  (STA)
            00000100 ⎫
            00000001 ⎭ location 260 (order reversed)
```

(The reasons for inverting the order of the address are discussed in the appropriate section of this chapter.) If, of course, you are fortunate enough to have an assembler supplied for your system, you can let that do the translation for you.

As mentioned in Chapter 2, if you have to work in machine code, it is a great help to accurate programming to write and check the program in assembly language first, before converting the instructions into binary and hexadecimal for entry through the keyboard or switches.

Examples in this chapter will be confined to the four most common microprocessor chips you are likely to encounter, either in building your own equipment or in using a packaged system. The chips (followed by some of the packaged systems they support) are: Intel 8080 (Altair and Imsai); Motorola 6800 (SWTP and MSI); MCS6502 (Apple and Pet); and Zilog Z-80 (Tandy TRS80 and Research Machines). These have many likenesses; all have 40 pins and work on eight bit operands, and there is much common ground in their instruction sets.

Some fundamentals

1. Notation

The binary and hexadecimal notations are described on page 22. Sometimes addresses or program listings are given in *octal*. This uses base 8. The decimal numbers 1−10 in octal are:

   1   2   3   4   5   6   7   10   11   12

2. Byte

All the microcomputers discussed use an eight-bit unit known as a *byte* as a unit of storage and as the basic instruction length.

3. Address

An *address* is the identifying number of a memory byte (a 'memory location') that holds data or an instruction. The example in the previous section referred to data held in address 260.

Although an address refers to a single byte, addresses in microcomputer systems are themselves usually two bytes (16 bits) long, so that locations with addresses larger than 255 can be referenced. Theoretically the largest address that can be held in two bytes is 65 535, but your system probably has much less than this amount of memory.

A system's memory is often referred to as having a certain number of 'K', where K stands for 1024 bytes; so a 32K system will have 32 768 locations, with addresses ranging from 0 to 32 767. Note that the first 256 locations of memory are often described as *page 0* of the memory.

If you are using assembly language, there is a facility ORG by which you can set the starting address of the program, e.g.

ORG 2000

would start assembling at address 2000.

You have to ensure that the addresses you choose for the storage of your programs and data do not interfere with those used by any monitor or input-output subroutine you are holding in memory at the same time as your program.

4. Registers

These are used for holding data and for some special purposes. Since they are an integral part of the microprocessor chip, access to them is much faster than to memory locations. They should therefore be used, when they are not being utilised for a special purpose, for the storage of intermediate results.

All four microprocessor systems have the following registers:

- program counter (shows address of next instruction);
- stack pointer (purpose explained on page 104);
- accumulator or A register (8 bits).

Other registers are:

8080	6800	6502	Z-80
General purpose			
B, C	B, C	None	B, C
D, E, H, L			D, E, H, L,
			A', B', C', D', E', H', L'

8080	6800	6502	Z-80

Special-purpose

None	Index register X	Index registers X, Y	IX, IY
			Interrupt vector
			Memory refresher

The use of the special-purpose registers will be explained in the course of this chapter.

5. Flags

A flag is a bit that defines a specific condition (e.g. arithmetic overflow in the accumulator) as true or false. It is given the value 1 if the condition is present and 0 if not. Flags are mostly concerned with arithmetic and interrupts, and are discussed in the relevant sections of this and the next chapter.

Transferring data

Some of the most important instructions deal with moving data from registers to memory locations and vice versa. Arithmetic is done in the accumulator, so a transfer to that register is needed. Temporary results are often moved from register to memory, while input-output usually needs a memory-to-register transfer.

Transfers between memory and accumulator

To perform arithmetic, one of the operands needs to be loaded into the accumulator using an LDA instruction (or equivalent), and the result needs to be stored using an instruction of the STA type. Appropriate instructions for the four microprocessors are given below. With these, as with the instructions given in other sections of this chapter, you should look up the length of the instruction, the flags (if any) affected, and the machine-code format on your code card.

8080

LDA   Loads the accumulator with the *contents* of the address given in the two bytes following the operation code. The low-order part of the address comes before the high-order; this does not affect your naming the address with a name of your choice in assembly language, but if you are working in machine code it is important to get this order right (see STA example on page 85).

LDAX B   Loads the accumulator with the *contents* of the address given in registers B and C. This enables you to use the same instruction to refer to a different address, simply by changing the register contents.

LDAX D   As above, but using registers D and E.

STA   Stores the contents of the accumulator in the address given in the two bytes following the operation code. Corresponds to LDA.

STAX B and STAX D correspond to LDAX B and LDAX D.

6800

CLR   Sets a memory location to zero.

CLRA   Sets the accumulator to zero.

LDAA   Loads the accumulator with the *contents* of the address given in the two bytes following the operation code. The high-order part of the address comes before the low-order (not as in the 8080); if the address is in the range 0–255 only one byte is needed to store it (this facility applies to *all* instructions containing a memory address). Can also load a *value* into the accumulator: the value is usually preceded by the # sign, e.g. LDAA # 5, and is held in the second byte of the instruction. This form of addressing is known as *immediate addressing*.

STAA   The 'store' command corresponding to LDAA.

6502

LDA and STA are like the 6800 LDAA and STAA, except that representation of an address in two bytes is 'back to front', as in the 8080.

Z-80

LD A, (location address or name)   Functions like the 8080 LDA.
LD (location address or name), A   Functions like the 8080 STA.
LD A, (BC)   Functions like the 8080 LDAX B.
LD A, (DE)   Functions like the 8080 LDAX D.
LD (BC), A   'Store' command, reverse of LD A, (BC).
LD (DE), A   'Store' command, reverse of LD A, (DE).

Be careful about the comma and brackets in all these instructions.

A program using some of the above instructions to interchange the contents of two memory locations, named COX and BOX, is given below. The 'load' instructions do not affect the contents of the memory location that they transfer to the accumulator, and the 'store' instructions do not affect the contents of the location transferred.

8080	*6800*	*6502*	*Z-80*
LDA COX	LDAA COX	LDA COX	LD A, (COX)
STA DUMP	STAA DUMP	STA DUMP	LD (DUMP), A
LDA BOX	LDAA BOX	LDA BOX	LD A, (BOX)
STA COX	STAA COX	STA COX	LD (COX), A
LDA DUMP	LDAA DUMP	LDA DUMP	LD A, (DUMP)
STA BOX	STAA BOX	STA BOX	LD (BOX), A

Transfer of data involving other registers

8080

LHLD	Loads registers L and H *respectively* with the contents of two memory locations: the address given in the two bytes following the operation code, and that address plus one. This is useful for transferring an address to L and H.
SHLD	Stores the contents of registers L and H in a pair of consecutive memory locations.
XCHG	Exchanges the contents of the register pairs D, E and H, L.
MOV R1, R2	Moves the contents of register R2 to register R1. For example, MOV A, E would transfer the contents of register E to the accumulator (counted as register A).
MOV M, R	Moves the contents of a register to the memory location *defined by the address stored in registers L and H*. For example, MOV M, A would transfer the contents of the accumulator to the address given in registers L and H.
MOV R, M	Reverses the above process, i.e. moves the contents of a memory location to a register. For example, MOV A, M would transfer to the accumulator the contents of the address given in registers L and H.
LXI RP	Loads a register pair (BC, DE, HL) with the value of the two bytes following the operation code. For example, LXI B, COX would load registers B and C with the address of COX.

| MVI M | Moves the value of the byte following the operation code into the memory location specified by the registers L and H. For example, MVI M, 7 would put 7 into the appropriate address. |
| MVI R | As above, but moves the value to a register instead of a memory location. For example, MVI A, 6 would put 6 in the accumulator. |

6800

LDAB	Loads register B with the contents of the address given in the two bytes following the operation code.
STAB	The corresponding store instruction.
TAB	Transfers the contents of the accumulator to register B.
TBA	The reverse of the above process.
LDX	Loads the index register with the contents of two memory locations: the address given in the two bytes following the operation code, and that address plus one.
STX	The corresponding store instruction.
TPA	Puts all flags into the accumulator.

6502

LDX	Loads index register X from memory locations (as 6800 LDX).
STX	The corresponding store instruction.
TAX	Puts the contents of the accumulator into register X.
TXA	Puts the contents of X into the accumulator.

LDY, STY, TAY, TYA are the corresponding instructions for index register Y.

Z-80

The following are the most common transfer instructions.

LD R1, R2	Loads the contents of register R2 into R1. R1 and R2 can be any of the registers A–E, H and L.
LD R, *n*	*n* is the *value* in the byte following the operation code. For example, LD A, 0 would clear the accumulator.
LD R, (HL)	Loads the contents of the address defined in registers H and L into a specified register. For example, LD C, (HL) would put the contents of the address defined in registers H and L into register C.
LD (HL), R	The reverse of the previous instruction.
LD (HL), *n*	Loads the contents of the byte following the operation code into the address defined in registers H and L.

LD A, (BC) ⎫
LD (BC), A ⎪   Similar to LD R, (HL) and LD (HL), R. They load or
LD A, (DE) ⎬   store the accumulator from the address specified by the
LD (DE), A ⎭   registers DE or BC.

LD HL, *nn*   Loads the two bytes after the operation code into the
H and L registers. Similar instructions are LD BC, *nn*
and LD DE, *nn*.

Addition and subtraction

Only addition and subtraction have instructions provided. Multiplication and division have to be performed by subroutines, which you can usually obtain easily.

The simplest type of arithmetic is in binary, involving two single-byte whole-number items. This forms the basis for arithmetic on larger numbers.

Binary notation has already been described in Chapter 2. The representation of negative numbers, however, was not discussed there. In most applications you are bound to meet negative amounts (such as a debit or a low temperature), and if you have a system that displays the contents of registers and memory in lights above switches you may encounter a negative number displayed. In binary, negative numbers are represented by 'twos complement' notation. This uses the most significant digit (the extreme left) of a binary number as the 'sign digit' to indicate whether the number is positive or negative. The sign digit is 0 for a positive number and 1 for a negative one. This limits the largest positive number you can hold in a single byte to 127 (01111111), and the largest negative number to −128 (10000000).

To find the negative representation of a positive number there are two methods:

1. Change 0s to 1s and 1s to 0s, then add 1. For example:

     +7 = 00000111
     −7 = 11111001

2. Subtract from 2 raised to the power of the number of bits in the representation you are using. If you are using one byte this will be 2^8 or 256; if two bytes, 2^{16} or 65 536. For example:

     256 − 7 = 249
     so   −7 = 11111001

You can check your conversion by adding the positive number and its negative conversion; they should equal zero in the number of bits you are using for number representation, e.g.

	+7	00000111
plus	−7	11111001

(1)00000000

The above two methods will also give you the positive equivalent of any negative number you may see in your lights in binary, e.g.

11110011
Reverse, and add one: 00001101 = 13

Therefore the number was −13. Some other negative representations in a single byte are:

−1	11111111
−3	11111101
−4	11111100
−64	11000000

Results from addition and subtraction are usually in the accumulator. All four systems can add the value of the byte following the operation code, so if an instruction is (on the 8080):

ADI 20

it would add 20 to the accumulator; 20 is known as the *immediate operand*.

All four systems have a *carry flag* (flags were briefly discussed on page 87). The carry flag is set to 1 if a carry (or borrow) occurs and cleared if this does not happen. All systems discussed except the 6502 have separate instructions for addition and subtraction with and without the contents of the carry flag being added to (or subtracted from) the result. It is useful in multi-precision arithmetic, which is discussed later in this section. The add and subtract instructions are as follows.

8080

ADI, ACI	Adds the contents of the byte following the operation code to the accumulator − with and without carry respectively.
SUI, SBI	The subtract form of the above − with or without borrow.
ADD R, ADC R	Adds the contents of a register to the accumulator − with or without carry.

SUB R, SBB R	The subtract form of the above – with or without borrow.
ADD M, ADC M	Adds the contents of a memory location referenced by the L and H registers – with or without carry.
SUB M, SBB M	The subtract form of the above – with or without borrow.

6800

ADDA, ADCA	Adds an immediate operand or the contents of a memory location to the accumulator – with or without carry.
SUBA, SBCA	The corresponding subtract instructions.
ADDB, ADCB $\}$ SUBB, SBCB $\int$	Perform the same functions using register B instead of the accumulator.
ABA, SBA	Adds/subtracts the contents of register B to/from the accumulator, with the result remaining in the accumulator.

6502

| ADC, SBC | Adds/subtracts an immediate operand or the contents of a memory location to/from the accumulator, with carry. CLC will clear the carry flag, if you wish to ensure that no carry influences the result. |

Z-80

ADD *n*, ADC *n*, SUB *n*, SBC *n* (where *n* is an immediate operand) are like 8080 ADI, ACI, SUI, SBI.

ADD *r*, ADC *r*, SUB *r*, SBC *r* correspond to the ADD R type of 8080 instruction.

ADD (HL), ADC (HL), SUB (HL), SBC (HL) correspond to the ADD M type of 8080 instruction.

The following example finds the difference between two variables CAT and DOG, and then adds 10 and 20. It is assumed that all numbers and the resulting sum can be held in a single byte. The carry facility is not used. To avoid this on the 6502 it is necessary to *set* the carry on a subtraction and *clear* it before an addition. On the other systems a variety of different instructions are utilised to show their use – hence this small program is not necessarily the most efficient way of performing the calculation. The 8080 and Z-80 programs both have to move a sum into a register and the address of a memory location to registers H and L before doing the calculation.

8080	6800	6502	Z-80
MVI B, 10	LDAB # 10	LDA CAT	LD B, 10
LXI H, DOG	LDAA CAT	SEC	LD HL, DOG
LDA CAT	SUBA DOG	SBC DOG	LD A, (CAT)
SUB M	ABA	CLC	SUB (HL)
ADD B	ADDA # 20	ADC # 10	ADD B
ADI 20		ADC # 20	ADD 20

If you are working in assembly language, as opposed to writing a program in this language and then converting it yourself to machine code, you may find the following facilities useful for calculation programs. EQU enables you to give a value to a variable before it is used in a program instruction. This facility is convenient for defining frequently used constants, e.g.

DOZEN EQU 12

DB has a similar function (and is sometimes written as DEFB), e.g.

DOZEN DB 12

DS reserves storage of a specified number of bytes for a data name, e.g.

QUANT DS 4

would reserve four bytes.

Multi-precision arithmetic

You will not want to be limited to quantities not greater than 127. The 8080 and Z-80 have instructions for two-byte arithmetic in registers. If you wish to work with quantities larger than that, you have to make use of the 'carry' facility in such instructions as ADC.

The 8080 two-byte add instruction is DAD followed by B, D or H, which adds to the registers H and L the contents of the register pairs BC, DE and HL. The first-named register in each case would contain the sign bit (0 if positive, 1 if negative) and the most significant part of the number. The equivalent Z-80 instruction is:

ADD HL, BC (or the corresponding register pair)

The following instructions add two 16-bit (two-byte) numbers in QUANT1 and QUANT2 and leave the result in registers H and L. The carry flag is set if there is a carry from the most significant bit.

8080	Z-80
LHLD QUANT1	LD BC, (QUANT1)
XCHG	LD HL, (QUANT2)
LHLD QUANT2	ADD HL, BC
DAD D	

If you have not the above systems, or want to use operands larger than two bytes, you will have to utilise the 'carry' version of the add and subtract instructions. The following example shows how addition and subtraction with carry operate on two 16-bit quantities.

Addition

(more significant byte)	(less significant byte)	
00011100	01110111	7 287
+01011111	11111100	+24 572
+ 1 carry flag	01110011	31 859
01111100		

Subtraction

00000100	00000000	1024
−00000000	10000000	−(+128)
− 1 carry flag	10000000	+896
00000011		

The first add or subtract must be done without carry (except on the 6502 when the carry flag must be cleared or set).

The following sequence of instructions performs COX + BOX = FOX on two-byte amounts. It is assumed that all results can be held in two bytes. In order to access the low-order byte of the operands, the address of the type 'COX + 1' is used. The high-order byte would be in COX and the low-order byte would be in the next address, which can be referred to as COX + 1; for example, if the number was 256:

COX	COX + 1
00000001	00000000

In machine code these are two contiguous addresses such as 300 and 301.

8080	*6800*	*6502*	*Z-80*
LDA COX + 1	LDAB COX + 1	CLC	LD A, (COX + 1)
MOV B, A	LDAA COX	LDA COX + 1	LD B, A
LDA BOX + 1	ADDB BOX + 1	ADC BOX + 1	LD A, (BOX + 1)
ADD B	ADCA BOX	STA FOX + 1	ADD A, B
STA FOX + 1	STAA FOX	LDA COX	LD (FOX + 1), A
LDA COX	STAB FOX + 1	ADC BOX	LD A, (COX)
MOV B, A		STA FOX	LD B, A
LDA BOX			LD A, (BOX)
ADC B			ADC A, B
STA FOX			LD (FOX), A

All systems except the 8080 have an *overflow flag*, which is set when a nine-bit signed number appears as a result of adding *two one-byte numbers with the same sign*. This condition occurs with negative numbers in the range -129 to -256 and positive ones in the range 128 to 254. It is usually an error condition.

So far it has been assumed that you are adding and subtracting whole numbers. You can assume the binary point at any place in a single or multi-precision number. For example, 00011110 could represent 7.5; here the point is assumed before the last two bits of the byte. Binary fractions descend in powers of two: $.1 = .5; .01 = .25; .001 = .125$ etc. You have to work out how many places of binary fractions your result needs, allowing for any multiplication and division, which respectively increase and decrease the number of significant figures in the result. It is best to divide all your input by the appropriate power of 2, so that it is all in fractional form. This power is known as a *scaling factor*. You will have to make adjustments each time you use a multiplication or division subroutine, if you wish to keep the original scaling, and then make the appropriate adjustment to the original numbers on output. This 'hunting the binary point' is a tiresome chore and is best avoided. *Floating point* routines that automatically handle these problems have been written for most systems, and should be used if you are working with fractional numbers. Alternatively, you can use the *binary-coded decimal* (BCD) form of number representation, where you have no need to worry about the lack of correspondence between the decimal point and the binary point. This very useful alternative to working in pure binary will now be discussed.

Binary-coded decimal addition and subtraction

BCD represents each digit of a decimal number as its binary equivalent in four bits ranging from 0 (0000) to 9 (1001). Two BCD values can be held in a single byte. Some examples of this form of number representation are:

```
 5 = 0000 0101   (0  5)
17 = 0001 0111   (1  7)
42 = 0100 0010   (4  2)
99 = 1001 1001   (9  9)
```

99 is the maximum value that can be held in a single byte, but larger numbers can be dealt with by multi-precision addition and subtraction. The decimal point can be assumed wherever you wish.

BCD is a relatively inefficient way of holding data, since more bits are used than with the corresponding binary representation. It is useful, however, in converting input characters from their format, if you are interfacing to instruments such as digital voltmeters, and if you are working with fractional numbers.

Addition and subtraction automatically give BCD results from BCD numbers if you employ the 'decimal adjust' instruction (DAA) after each add or subtract on the 8080, 6800 and Z-80. This affects the 'auxiliary carry' or 'half-carry' flag: AC on the 8080, H on the 6800, H (and N if it is a subtract instruction) on the Z-80. All the previously described add and subtract instructions can be used, both with and without carry. The carry forms are used if you wish to work with more than two BCD digits.

On the 6502 the decimal flag is set by the SED and cleared by the CLD instruction. Once set, all subsequent adds and subtracts are done in BCD until the flag is cleared.

The following sequence of statements computes PRICE1 + PRICE2 − DISCT for the four systems. It assumes that no values are going to be greater than 99.

8080	6800	6502	Z-80
LDA PRICE1	LDAA PRICE1	CLC	LD A, (PRICE1)
MOV B, A	ADDA PRICE2	SED	LD B, A
LXI H, DISCT	DAA	LDA PRICE1	LD HL, DISCT
LDA PRICE2	SUBA DISCT	ADC PRICE2	LD A, (PRICE2)
ADD B	DAA	SEC	ADD A, B
DAA		SBC DISCT	DAA
SUB M			SUB (HL)
DAA			DAA

9

Further assembly-language and machine-code facilities

So far only programs without branches and loops have been discussed. This chapter describes the assembly-language method of handling these, and introduces some further useful features. The appropriate machine-code operation codes can be derived from a code card.

Branching

This facility enables you to go to a certain part of a program if a certain flag condition (set by an arithmetic or compare instruction) is true, and to continue obeying instructions in their normal order if it is false. The following short sequence of instructions for the 8080 continues with the program if the addition has produced a positive result (using the JP instruction to a label NEXT) and stops (using the HLT instruction) if the result is not positive.

    ADD B
    JP NEXT
    HLT
    NEXT
    (rest of program)

The branching instructions of the 6800 and 6502 work only with *relative addresses*, and this form can also be used with the Z-80. In this form of addressing, the second byte of the instruction has the number of bytes (the number can be positive or negative) that are to be added to the program counter in order to find the address to which the program must branch if the tested condition is true. Using the positive bit-test (BPL) of the 6800, the instruction:

    400 BPL 4

would go to the instruction in address 406 if the condition were true. Since a branch instruction on the 6800 and 6502 is two bytes long, the program counter would be set to 402 when the branch instruction was being obeyed; the value 4 would be added to this — hence the address of 406. The rule is to add (2 + number in immediate operand) to calculate the effective address. The immediate operand must be within the range −128 to +127, since it must be contained in a single byte. This means that the address to which the program branches if the condition is true must be within the range −126 to +129 bytes away from the branch instruction.

Many assemblers allow you to put a label after the branch instruction to specify the address to which you wish to branch, e.g.

BPL NEXT

You will find this form in many published listings of 6800 and 6502 programs. This relieves you of the tedium of working out the operand of a relative branch instruction, since this chore is done by the assembler. If you are working in machine code, however, you will have to insert a positive or negative number as the immediate operand.

Below are some useful branch instructions for the four systems.

8080	6800	6502	Z-80		
JC	BCS	BCS	JP C, address	(or JR C, i)	Branch if carry set
JNC	BCC	BCC	JP NC,	(or JR NC, i)	Branch if no carry
JM	BMI	BMI	JP M,		Branch if sign flag = 1
JP	BPL	BPL	JP P,		Branch if sign flag = 0
JZ	BEQ	BEQ	JP Z,	(or JR Z, i)	Branch if zero flag = 1
JNZ	BNE	BNE	JP NZ,	(or JR NZ, i)	Branch if zero flag = 0

The JR forms of Z-80 instructions use relative addresses (i), like the 6800. The 6800 has also got the instructions:

BLT   Branch if sign + overflow = 1
BLE   Branch if zero or sign + overflow = 1
BLS   Branch if zero or carry = 1
BGE   Branch if sign + overflow = 0
BGT   Branch if zero and sign + overflow = 0
BHI   Branch if branch and carry = 0

If you are using signed values, BLT, BLE, BGE, BEQ and BNE are the appropriate 6800 instructions. If plain two-byte values, BCS, BLS, BCC, BHI, BEQ and BNE are the relevant instructions.

There is in all systems an *unconditional* branch instruction. This branches to the point in the program indicated, and obeys instructions in order from that point. Programs that leap about are difficult to correct and understand, so this instruction should be used sparingly − if at all. Its form is:

8080	JMP address
6800	BRA relative address or JMP address
6502	JMP address or JMP relative address
Z-80	JP address

The JMP instruction on the 6800 enables you to overcome any limitation imposed by the range of the relative address that can be held in a single byte. You can use any of the 6800 branch instructions to take you by means of the relative address to a JMP instruction, which can then take you out of the usual range. If you wish to branch as a result of comparing two operands, you can subtract them and then use the branch instruction to take you to the appropriate path. The following sequence of instructions goes to the label BIG if the contents of DOG > CAT, goes to LIKE if they are equal, and continues in sequence if CAT > DOG.

8080	6800	6502	Z-80
LDA CAT	LDAA DOG	SEC	LD A, (CAT)
MOV B, A	SUBA CAT	LDA DOG	LD B, A
LDA DOG	BEQ LIKE	SBC CAT	LD A, (DOG)
SUB B	BPL BIG	BEQ LIKE	SUB B
JZ LIKE		BPL BIG	JP Z, LIKE
JP BIG			JP P, BIG

The use of the 'compare' instruction enables you to make comparisons without a subtraction, and sets the appropriate flags so that you can use a branch instruction as a result of the flag settings. The forms of this instruction are as follows. *All set the appropriate flags.*

8080
CMP M compares the accumulator with the contents of an address specified (as you may have guessed from your reading of the previous chapter) by the contents of the H and L registers.
CMP R and CPI compare the accumulator with a register and an immediate operand respectively.

6800
CMPA and CMPB compare the contents of an address with the accumulator and register B respectively.
CBA compares the accumulator and register B.

6502
The contents of an address can be compared to the accumulator, X register and Y register by CMP, CPX and CPY respectively.

Z-80
CP (HL), CP R and CP *n* correspond to the three 8080 instructions.

Below is the 6800 sequence of instructions branching on a comparison of DOG and CAT rewritten using the compare instruction.

```
LDAA DOG
CMPA CAT
BEQ LIKE
BPL BIG
```

Loops

Most programs contain loops, as explained in Chapter 1. You have now met the standard way of programming a loop in which the number of items terminates with a 'sentinel' such as −1. You could use either subtraction or the compare instruction to test for equality of each item in turn with the sentinel.

You could also program a loop, if it deals with a fixed number of items, by keeping a count and testing it each time round the loop. This could have the disadvantage of using the accumulator, so you may have to store and re-store any other totals each time you augment or test the count.

All four systems have useful instructions for incrementing or decrementing a count in a register or memory location by 1 and setting the appropriate flags. These are useful for dealing with *arrays* (see pages 12−14) as well as counts. The appropriate forms are given below.

8080
INR M and DCR M: increments/decrements by 1 a count in a memory
    location defined by registers H and L.
INR R and DCR R: as above, for a register.

6800
INCA, DECA, INCB, DECB, INC, DEC, INX and DEX perform the
    above operations for the accumulator, register B, memory location
    and register X respectively.

6502
The above operations are performed on a memory location and registers
    X and Y by INC, DEC, INX, DEX, INY and DEY respectively.

Z-80
INC (HL), DEC (HL), INC R and DEC R correspond to the above 8080
    instructions.

The following program uses a loop to multiply the contents of ITEM by five (in a relatively inefficient way, although it shows the use of looping methods). A test is made of a count to ascertain if it is non-zero after each decrement. If it is, the loop is obeyed once more. The accumulator is put to zero at the start of the program and the multiplication is performed by adding ITEM five times.

Alternative counts (such as a negative one) could have been set and alternative tests made. You should always ensure that the affirmative test of the condition will take you back to the start of the loop, and that when the condition is no longer true you continue immediately with the rest of the program. This saves unnecessary unconditional jumps. If you are programming the 6800 or 6502 in machine code, therefore, put a negative quantity in the immediate address of the test instruction, to jump backwards to the start of the loop.

8080	6800	6502	Z-80
MVI A, 0	CLRA	LDA # 0	LD A, 0
MVI B, 5	LDX # 5	LDX # 5	LD B, 5
LXI H, ITEM	ST ADDA ITEM	ST CLC	LD HL, ITEM
ST ADD M	DEX	ADC ITEM	ST ADD A, (HL)
DCR B	BGT ST	DEX	DEC B
JNZ ST		BNE ST	JP NZ ST

The start of the loop is labelled ST, and it is assumed that the product can be held in a single byte.

The 8080 and Z-80 have also increment and decrement instructions that affect a two-byte value in a register pair, but these do *not* change flags.

Arrays and tables

The idea of an array or table, where each element was identified by the table-name and a subscript indicating its position in the array (e.g. A_1, V_{18}), was described in Chapter 1. To translate flowcharts using arrays into machine-code or assembly-language programs you need to use a technique known as *indexed addressing*. This adds the contents of an index register to the contents of the address of certain instructions, so that by incrementing (or decrementing) the value of the index register you can go through a loop addressing a different array or table item each time. The 6800, 6502 and Z-80 have index registers known respectively as X, X and Y, IX and IY. All except those of the 6502 are 16 bits long. In the 6502, index register Y can only be used on page 0 addresses (0–255) with the LDX and STX instructions.

The forms of a typical instruction using an index register are:

6800	LDAA 2, X
6502	LDA TABLE, X
Z-80	LD(IX − 2), A

The item before the comma in the 6800 and Z-80 examples is known as the *displacement*.

The 8080 has no true index registers. The increment and decrement instructions that work with register pairs (such as the useful H, L) do not affect flags. If you are very careful and know the machine-code address (which, in assembly language, you can set by ORG, described on page 86) you can use INR L to decrease or increase register L if you are sure it will cause no carry. Alternatively, you can keep a separate count in a single register, such as B, and then use the INX H or DCX H to increment or decrement the register pair H and L. Similar techniques can be used with the Z-80.

The following sequence of instructions sums an array or table of 12 items in the starting address WEIGHT in the accumulator. It assumes that the total can be held in a single byte.

8080	6800	6502	Z-80
LXI H, WEIGHT	LDX # WEIGHT	LDX # − 12	LD HL, WEIGHT
MVI D, 12	CLRA	LDA #0	LD D, 12
MVI A, 0	LDAB # − 12	ST CLC	LD A, 0
ST ADD M	ST ADDA X	ADC TAB + 12, X	ST ADD A, (HL)
INX H	INX	INX	INC HL
DCR D	INC B	BMI ST	DEC D
JNZ ST	BMI ST		JP NZ, ST

Subroutines

Writing often-used sequences of instructions once in a program and being able to call them as many times as you wish was discussed in Chapter 1. Many useful subroutines for all four systems under review have been designed for such purposes as multi-precision and floating-point arithmetic and input and output.

In the 8080 subroutines are invoked by the CALL statement. There are some conditional forms of this also. CC, CM, CNC, CNZ, CP and CZ call on the respective conditions of carry, minus, no carry, no zero, positive and zero. The RET instruction transfers control to the next statement after the CALL etc. in the program that invoked the subroutine. There are conditional forms of RET (RC, RM etc.) corresponding to the conditional forms of the CALL and JMP instructions.

The 6800 has two call instructions: BSR (which must be followed by a *relative* address and so is limited in its range as described on page 99) and JSR (which uses a normal or indexed address). Return from a subroutine is made by the RTS statement.

The 6502 uses the JSR and RTS instructions.

The Z-80 CALL and the conditional forms CALL NZ address etc. correspond to the 8080 instructions, as do RET, RET NC etc. The following sequence of instructions uses a subroutine twice to multiply an amount by three.

8080	6800	6502	Z-80
LXI H, COX	LDAA COX	LDA COX	LD HL, COX
LDA BOX	ADDA BOX	CLC	LD A, (BOX)
ADD M	JSR TRIPLE	ADC BOX	ADD A, (HL)
CALL TRIPLE	STAA FOX	JSR TRIPLE	CALL TRIPLE
STA FOX	LDAA DOG	STA FOX	LD (FOX), A
LXI H, DOG	ADDA CAT	LDA DOG	LD HL, DOG
LDA CAT	JST TRIPLE	CLC	LD A, (CAT)
ADD M	STAA HOG	ADC CAT	ADD A, (HL)
CALL TRIPLE		JSR TRIPLE	CALL TRIPLE
STA HOG		STA HOG	LD (HOG), A
TRIPLE MOV B, A	TRIPLE TAB	TRIPLE STA TEMP	TRIPLE LD B, A
ADD A	ABA	CLC	ADD A, A
ADD A	ABA	ADC TEMP	RET
RET	RTS	CLC	
		ADC TEMP	
		RTS	

The above subroutine TRIPLE needs the item to be tripled to be placed in the accumulator and returns with the product in the same place. Except for the 6502, the contents of register B are overwritten. Published subroutines always give details of any registers or flags altered. If you are writing a very general-purpose subroutine yourself, it is as well to save vital registers and flags on entry to the subroutine and restore them just before exit. A method of performing this is described in the next section.

Stack operations

A *stack* is an area of memory where data is stored and retrieved on the 'last in, first out' (LIFO) principle. The most recent item added to the stack is said to be at the *top* of the stack. Instructions access the item(s) at the top of the stack. The stack of the 6502 is fixed and occupies addresses 100 to 1FF (hexadecimal), 256 bytes in all. In the other systems the programmer fixes the stack area.

All systems have a *stack pointer* (SP), which points to the *last used* stack location, i.e. top of stack. The 8080 and Z-80 stack pointer has to be initially loaded by the programmer with an *address value one greater* than the first stack location, since the stack pointer is always decremented by the instructions that store data in the stack. The appropriate instructions are as follows.

8080
LXI SP, address value (e.g. LXI SP, 4001) loads a value to the SP. SPHL transfers the contents of registers H and L to the stack pointer.

6800

Unlike the 8080, the stack pointer actually indicates the top of the stack; LDS is the appropriate instruction.

6502

The stack pointer is loaded from register X with TXS.

Z-80

LD SP, address value and LD SP, HL correspond to the 8080 instructions.

The stack is mainly used for:

● Automatic storage of the program counter (giving the point in the invoking program to which you wish to return) when a subroutine is called. The calling statement automatically decrements the stack pointer by 2 (since two bytes are needed to store the program counter) and increments it by 2 when the subroutine is left.

● Storage of registers and flags on entrance to a subroutine. You have to perform these actions yourself if you wish to use the stack in this way. The appropriate instructions are:

8080

The accumulator, flags (called PSW) and appropriate register pairs can
   be pushed or popped from the stack (and the appropriate adjustment
   made to the program counter) by PUSH A, PUSH PSW, PUSH B,
   PUSH D, PUSH H, POP A, POP PSW, POP B and POP D.
INX SP and DCX SP increment and decrement SP by 1.

6800

PSHA, PSHB, PULA and PULB perform the above actions with registers
   A and B.
INS and DES work like INX and DCX.

6502

The accumulator and flags can be pushed or pulled to stack and the
   program counter appropriately altered by PHA, PHP, PLA, PLP.

Z-80

PUSH AF and POP AF affect both the accumulator and the flags. Other
   instructions, which correspond to the 8080 ones, are PUSH BC,
   PUSH D, PUSH HL, POP BC, POP DE, POP HL, INC SP and DEC SP.

Every 'push' must have a corresponding 'pull'; if you are using the stack for temporary storage and have more than one exit from your sub-routine, you must ensure that the stack pointer is in the appropriate place for each RET (or equivalent) instruction. Comment on your coding sheet, and indentation of each level of push and pop, will assist you here.

Bit manipulation

Sometimes you wish to recognise the individual bits within a byte, e.g. if you are setting and testing your own flags and you wish to save space by having eight flags to a word. The systems under review have 'shift' and 'logical' instructions to assist you in this type of programming. Shifts are also useful in multiplication, and sometimes in division, and these instructions will now be discussed.

8080
All shifts are rotary shifts, i.e. each bit shifted out of one end of the word reappears at the other end.

	Before		*After*	
	Cy	Acc.	Cy	Acc.
RLC rotates accumulator one place left. Most significant bit goes into carry and rightmost end.	0	10101010	1	01010101
RRC is the corresponding right shift.	0	10101010	0	01010101
RAL treats accumulator and carry as nine bits and rotates accordingly.	0	10101010	1	01010100
RAR is the corresponding right shift.	0	10101010	0	01010101

6800

	Before		*After*	
	Cy	Acc.	Cy	Acc.
ROLA, ROLB, ROL shift the accumulator, B register or a memory location in the same way as 8080 RAL.				
ASLA, ASLB, ASL shift 'arithmetically' left. The carry takes the sign bit and a zero enters the rightmost end.	1	10101010	1	01010100
LSRA, LSRB, LSR are 'logical' right shifts. The sign bit becomes zero and the least significant bit enters the carry.	1	10101010	0	01010101

6502

The accumulator or a memory location can be shifted in rotation left, arithmetically left or logically right by the ROL, ASL and LSR instructions respectively. These function like the corresponding 6800 instructions.

Z-80

RLCA, RRCA, RLA and RRA act on the accumulator, and correspond to the 8080 shifts described above. All the shifts described below act on a register, or on a memory location accessed by an index register or registers H and L, e.g. RLCD, RLC(HL).

The following are rotary shifts like the ones discussed above: RL and RR perform nine-bit shifts (operand with carry), while RLC and RRC work on eight bits in a manner analogous to 8080 instructions of the same name.

SRL and SLA are 'logical' shifts (in spite of the fact that the latter is designated an arithmetic one): bits that are shifted out of the operand are lost (except that they set the carry flag), and zeros fill vacated bit positions. Their action is shown below:

	Before		After	
	Operand	Cy	Operand	Cy
SRL shifts right.	01010011	0	00101001	1

	Cy	Operand	Cy	Operand
SLA shifts left.	1	01010011	0	10100110

	Operand	Cy	Operand	Cy
SRA is an arithmetic shift since	01010101	0	00101010	1
the sign bit is repeated, as the	10101010	1	11010101	0

two adjacent examples show.
The least significant bit enters
the carry.

Rotary shifts are used primarily to align bits in a word, in conjunction with the AND and OR instructions described in the next section. As you will see, combining the various types of instruction allows you to erase bits from an operand and 'push' bits from another word into their place.

Logical shifts can be used for the same purpose. They also multiply by two (left shift) and divide by two (right shift), and so are useful in implementing subroutines for these purposes.

The arithmetic shift should not be used to align bits, because, if the sign digit in the original operand was 1, this would be repeated for each arithmetic right shift. It divides a number (consisting of seven bits and sign) by two, and preserves the quotient.

The Z-80 has also two shifts, RLD and RRD, which work on both a memory location (defined by registers H and L) and the lower half of the accumulator; the upper four bits of the accumulator are unaffected. RLD and RRD consider these 12 bits as consisting of three binary-coded decimal (BCD) digits. Their action is shown below.

	Before		*After*	
	Acc.	Location	Acc.	Location
RLD	12	34	13	42
RRD	12	34	14	23

Logical operations

If you wish to save part of a byte (for a flag or number) and store something from another byte or register in the other part, the shifts will assist you to position the preserved part of the byte. The logical instructions assist you to erase the unwanted bits and put the desired information into the vacant place.

There are three types of logical instruction. The 'logical arithmetic' they perform on a 0 bit and a 1 bit, and the effect of their use on a whole byte, are shown below.

AND (∧)

0	0	1	1		11100010
AND 0	AND 1	AND 0	AND 1	AND	01010101
0	0	0	1		01000000

This instruction is used mainly to mask out unwanted bits.

OR (inclusive OR) (∨)

0	0	1	1		11100010
OR 0	OR 1	OR 0	OR 1	OR	01010101
0	1	1	1		11110111

This is used chiefly to merge bits into a byte.

OR (exclusive OR, XOR) (⊕)

0	0	1	1		11100010
XOR 0	XOR 1	XOR 0	XOR 1	XOR	01010101
0	1	1	0		10110111

This is rarely used. If the contents of a register or byte are XORed with themselves, the register byte is cleared, e.g.

```
      10101010
XOR   10101010
      _____
      00000000
```

This is the quickest way of clearing an accumulator or register.

The forms of the three logical operations for the four systems are as follows.

8080

ANA R, ANA M, ANA I perform 'and' on the accumulator and the specified operand (R is a register, M is a memory location defined by registers H and L, and I is an immediate operand in the second byte of the instruction).

ORA M, ORA R, ORA I, XRA M, XRA R and XRA I are corresponding instructions for the other logical functions.

6800

The logical functions are performed on the contents of the accumulator or register B by the instructions ANDA, ANDB, ORAA, ORAB, EORA, EORB. The operand can be a memory location, an indexed address or an immediate operand.

6502

The logical functions are performed on the contents of a memory location or immediate operand and the contents of the accumulator by AND, ORA, EOR.

Z-80

AND R, AND (HL), AND N, OR R, OR (HL), OR N, XOR R, XOR (HL) and XOR N correspond to the 8080 instructions listed above.

Character representation

If you can obtain a character directly from an input device before it has been processed it is likely to be in the ASCII code (American Standard Code for Information Interchange), which represents all numbers, letters and special symbols in seven bits. (An eighth bit is often a *parity* bit, to indicate whether the byte has been corrupted in transmission. For example, the parity bit may be set or cleared, before transmission, to make the total number of 1s in the byte *even*. Then on receipt the number of 1s is counted: if it is odd the transmission must have been faulty.)

Conversion of code to numbers provides a useful example of the shift and logical instructions just described. Characters can be compared using the compare and branch instructions if you wish to perform processing on text. You must *not*, however, attempt to perform arithmetic on the ASCII forms of numbers.

ASCII numbers correspond closely to the BCD form. If you assume that the eighth (parity) bit of an ASCII character stored in a byte is 0, the ASCII and BCD equivalents of decimal digits are:

Decimal	ASCII	BCD
0	00110000	00000000
5	00110101	00000101
9	00111001	00001001

The following sequence of instructions examines a byte named STATUS to ascertain whether characters have been read in correctly. If the bit in the '8' position in STATUS (0000X000) is 1, the characters have not been read correctly and the program branches to a label FAULT. If reading is correct, two ASCII characters are inserted into addresses CHARA and CHARB. The sequence of instructions stores these in a byte named NUMBER in BCD form. The flag-word STATUS should not be destroyed. The B in the immediate operand after the logical instructions implies that this operand is in binary form.

8080	6800	6502	Z-80
LDA STATUS	LDAA STATUS	LDA STATUS	LD A, (STATUS)
ANI 00001000B	ANDA # 00001000B	AND # 00001000B	AND 00001000B
JNZ FAULT	BNE FAULT	BNE FAULT	JP NZ FAULT
LDXI H, NUMBER	LDAA NUMBER	LDA NUMBER	LD HL, NUMBER
LDA NUMBER	EORA NUMBER	EOR NUMBER	LD A, (NUMBER)
XRA M	STAA NUMBER	STA NUMBER	XOR (HL)
STA NUMBER	LDAA CHARA	LDA CHARA	LD (NUMBER), A
LDA CHARA	ANDA # 00001111B	AND # 00001111B	LD A, (CHARA)
ANI 00001111	ASLA	ASL	AND 00001111
RLC	ASLA	ASL	RLCA
RLC	ASLA	ASL	RLCA
RLC	ASLA	ASL	RLCA
RLC	STAA NUMBER	STA NUMBER	RLCA
STA NUMBER	LDAA CHARB	DLA CHARB	LD (NUMBER), A
LDA CHARB	ANDA # 00001111B	AND # 00001111B	LD A, (CHARB)
ANDA 00001111B	ORAA NUMBER	ORA NUMBER	AND 00001111
ORA M	STAA NUMBER	STA NUMBER	OR (HL)
STA NUMBER			LD (NUMBER), A

Input and output

The simple storage of two BCD characters from two memory locations will give you some indication of what is involved in the transfer of data to and from input and output devices *after* it has been put in a memory location.

The problem above dealt only with a couple of BCD digits and assumed nothing about erroneous characters, redundant characters (e.g. space), negative numbers, binary or floating-point numbers, or the process required to transfer a character from a device such as a keyboard, paper-tape reader or floppy disc to a memory location.

Input and output devices are by no means standardised, and you are very strongly advised to take the subroutines for input and output supplied for a particular device or obtainable from published sources. If these do not contain character conversion to the arithmetical forms (binary, BCD, floating point) you wish to use, there are numerous published subroutines for the conversion of ASCII characters to these forms. Programming an input-output routine, especially for a complex peripheral device such as a floppy disc or a VDU, is only for the virtuoso programmer. Many monitors contain input and output systems for the standard peripherals they use.

Data transfer to and from slow peripherals such as a keyboard, paper-tape reader or typewriter is done character by character. This is known as *programmed input-output*. It would be too slow for fast peripherals such as floppy discs and some VDUs, where block transfers of characters are performed using a technique known as *direct memory access* (DMA). The actual transfer of the block is done automatically without programmer intervention.

Whether DMA is used or not, the program has to perform the task of converting each character and testing the *status word* of the device to see whether it is 'ready' or 'busy', or whether any fault has occurred during transmission.

Conversion is done before the transmission of an output character and after transmission of a character from an input device. Spaces, new lines (carriage returns), decimal points and other punctuation have to be taken into account.

A bit in the device's status word enables the programmer to determine whether the device is still busy in transferring the previous character or block. If the bit is not set, the program may be arranged to loop round until the device is ready for transfer. Other bits in the status word are used to give information on any fault that may occur, such as a parity error or end-of-tape condition in a cassette reader. Some bits also perform a control function, such as starting or stopping the cassette recorder. If the status is satisfactory the transfer of data by DMA or programmed input-output can proceed.

As an alternative to looping until the device is ready for a transfer of data, the system can be programmed so that whatever is being processed will automatically be *interrupted* (using the interrupt facility described in the next section) when the device is ready. This enables other processing to take place between transfers, and is vital if, in addition to working with an input-output device, you are also controlling an external device where the process cannot always be suspended for the time it may take to keep in the 'ready'-testing loop. If interrupts are allowed (they would be disallowed during the part of the program that was vital to control of the external device) the program will obey the input-output routine whenever a device is ready.

Interrupts

As outlined above, the interrupt facility enables a program to be interrupted automatically to attend to the needs of an input-output device. Only a small portion of the 2 milliseconds between the appearance of successive characters on a high-speed paper-tape reader is taken up by the actual processing of the character, usually about 3 microseconds. The interrupted program can then be resumed until the next interrupt occurs.

Interrupts are also useful in forcing entry into a section of program to correct some *urgent* condition (such as the switching of points in a model railway) or to display a message of an alarming condition such as exceeding maximum required temperature in a central-heating control system. They can also be used in connection with the clock, to interrupt automatically at predetermined intervals of time to attend to some condition.

An interrupt flag enables interrupts to be recognised or ignored. All systems under review except the 8080 have a *non-maskable* interrupt, which cannot be ignored and which can be used in connection with vital functions.

When interrupt occurs, unless it is decided to ignore it, the program proceeds to a predetermined address and obeys instructions from that point. The program counter is stored on entry to the interrupt program and restored when the routine is finished, as with entry and exit to a subroutine. Interrupt routines should be written in a section of memory where they cannot be entered by accident, and should be carefully constructed if processing has to take place in a very small amount of time. The interrupt facilities of the four systems are briefly discussed below.

8080

EI enables interrupts to be entered; DI disables (i.e. inhibits) such entry. Usually on entry to an interrupt routine you disable interrupts until that interrupt routine has been finished. The RET instruction is used when you wish to return to the main program from an interrupt routine, as you did when programming subroutines.

There may be up to eight devices that can cause interrupt. The starting addresses for the interrupt routines of these devices are 0, 8, 16, 24, 32, 40, 48 and 56. Since it is not likely that the whole interrupt processing can be performed in eight bytes, the starting address for a particular interrupt usually jumps to an area of memory containing the appropriate subroutine. A piece of hardware known as a priority interrupt module or control unit is used if you wish to set levels of priority among the devices that can cause interrupt. This will organise priority if there are simultaneous interrupt requests.

When interrupt is allowed, an RST instruction is jammed on the data bus. This saves the program counter *only*, before entering the interrupt routine at one of the above addresses. You have to take action yourself at the start of the interrupt routine if you want to save any registers and flags in the stack or memory area, and (in most cases) if you want to set the interrupt disable flag. At the end of appropriate processing you then have to take action to restore the original contents of registers and flags and set the interrupt enable flag, before ending with a RET instruction. This will return to the point where you left the main program.

6800

The interrupt 'mask' (as the flag is called) is enabled by the instruction SEI and disabled by CLI. SWI is an instruction that allows interrupt by program, instead of by an external device; it transfers control to an address stored in the hexadecimal memory locations FFFA and FFFB, which is the first instruction of the routine dealing with this type of interrupt. As in all types of 6800 interrupt under discussion, the contents of accumulator, register B, index register and flags as well as the program counter are preserved in the stack and restored on exit. Exit is done by the RTI instruction.

The non-maskable interrupt (NMI) is only used in powerdown conditions.

The single allowed interrupt from an external device goes to memory locations FFF8 and FFF9 (hexadecimal) to get the starting address of the routine to deal with the interrupt. The preservation of registers and flags and the use of the RTI instruction occur as with the software interrupt, SWI. If interrupts are desired from more than one external device, the interrupt signals are ORed together; then after interrupt occurs the status bit of each device is examined to see which caused the interrupt.

6502

The interrupt flag is set by SEI and cleared by CLI.

The instruction for the start of the routine dealing with the non-maskable interrupt is stored in memory locations FFFA and FFFB. The program counter and flags alone are stored. Return is accomplished by RTI.

The external interrupt program starts in locations FFFE and FFFF. Only the program counter and flags are stored. If you wish to have more than one device capable of interrupt you must adopt the technique described for the 6800 above.

Z-80

The Z-80 has three modes of maskable interrupt — set by the instructions IM0, IM1 and IM2 — in addition to a non-maskable interrupt. When the latter occurs the program counter is saved in the stack, and control is transferred to the start of the routine to deal with the interrupt, which is stored in memory location 0066 (hexadecimal). Other interrupts are automatically disabled while the routine is being obeyed. Return is done by an RETN instruction.

Interrupt mode 0 is like the 8080 interrupt system discussed above. Return is accomplished by a RETI instruction.

Interrupt mode 1 is similar to the non-maskable interrupt, except that it can be ignored if the interrupt flag is disabled by a DI instruction, and the starting address of the single program allowed is at hexadecimal memory location 0038. Return is by the RETI instruction.

In mode 2 some 128 interrupt routines are possible. The starting address for each one of these is stored in an address made up of the high-order byte from the *interrupt vector register* (which you load with LD I, A) and the low-order byte supplied by the device causing the interrupt. If the interrupt vector (or I) register contained FF and the device supplied 16, you would find the address of the routine to process this interrupt in hexadecimal location FF16. These addresses are usually held together in an interrupt vector table, which can contain 128 entries. When entering a mode 2 interrupt routine, only the program counter is stored in the stack. Exit is accomplished by the RETI instruction.

10

Program development and testing

If you write any program but the simplest it is unlikely to work when you first enter it through the keyboard or switches. There is no need at all to be disillusioned about this. A standard US industry speed for assembly-language programming of microcomputers was ten fully tested instructions daily. In a high-level language, one leading British user of computers assesses the average programmer output at 21 statements per day, while a mainframe computer manufacturer estimates a daily output of 15 statements.

You will find that the emphasis on documentation of programs, mentioned at the end of Chapter 1, is important when it comes to testing the program. Testing begins with the flowchart. The various levels of flowchart should be connected with your instructions in whatever programming language you are using. In the case of assembly language or machine code you may need to have an extra level of flowchart that connects those very detailed instructions with the logical steps of the task you wish to perform. If the first box in your outline flowchart is lettered A, all breakdowns of the logical steps and program instructions to perform the task declared in that box should have a starting reference of A.

If you are working in a commercial or educational microcomputer system installation you should try to have your flowchart checked by someone else with a knowledge of programming, as you can become so absorbed in your own creation that you are blinded to obvious errors of logic.

Time spent on testing the flowchart is amply repaid by the considerable lessening of the time that will be spent in front of the keyboard or switches in testing the actual program. In most problems you will be able to find data to which you already know the answer, to test your proposed flowchart solution (only a few simulation and operational-research problems are likely to baffle you). If you are programming a game you may have to test the program by actually dealing out a hand of cards or throwing a die at appropriate points.

When testing a flowchart you need to head a sheet of paper with the names of all variables (such as weight, count and total in the problem discussed in Chapter 1) and insert changed values after every step in the flowchart. You will also have to have a column for every decision in the program and insert 'yes' or 'no' at each test (as in the worked example on page 9). Work through every step, altering values in the columns where appropriate. You may need to use a calculator if complicated computation is involved.

Some other guidelines in the hand-checking of flowcharts are:

● Use small amounts of data, as in the example in Chapter 1 when a loop that is meant to be obeyed 12 times is tested with only three items.
● Ensure that each path in the program (including error conditions) is tested. A generalised income tax routine, for instance, should cover all bands of income as well as week 1 and emergency coding.
● If you are testing a file updating program, use a small file containing an example of each type of record.
● If you are writing a program for a business application, consult the appropriate user department to see that you have catered for all possible alternatives and combinations of data and for all likely error conditions: their experience of these is likely to be greater than yours. Checking the flowchart is likely to reveal some error conditions for which you have not catered.
● Ensure that you include messages to the operator with regard to the type and number of items to be entered at the keyboard, or the time to insert a new cassette file. This is a worthwhile precaution even if you are likely to be the only person using the program, as after a lapse of time you may forget some of these factors.

Stages in testing a coded program

After the flowchart has been checked for logical accuracy, it will be coded or translated into the instructions of the programming language you are using. To ease the testing of the program, and to assist you if you should wish to alter it after the program is fully operational, it is advisable to divide it (if the program length warrants it) into self-contained sections of no more than 50 instructions or statements. This is known to the profession as *modular programming*. Certain variables or locations will be reserved for passing data from one module to another. Sometimes there is a case for writing the whole program as a series of subroutines, so that the main program in Basic would consist entirely of GOSUB statements and in Fortran of CALL statements and in machine code and assembly language by the various CALL and JSR instructions. The BREAK instruction, which is found in some monitors such as the Zilog MCB monitor, can be used at appropriate points in an assembly-language program to halt the execution of the program so that appropriate registers and address-contents can be examined.

If you are using a program that you have not written yourself it may need some 'tailoring' before it can be adapted to your own system. If the alterations are extensive, it will need the same amount of testing as if you had written the program yourself. Any Basic program written for a microprocessor configuration different from your own (or for a minicomputer or mainframe) will need careful examination: it may use facilities (such as functions and statements) not provided in your own version of Basic, and may even use some abbreviations for statements (such as P for PRINT) that cannot be transferred to another system. In some cases you may have to consult the programming manual of the system for which the program was originally written to ascertain the meaning of an abbreviation or the exact working of a strange function or statement. Fortran programs are more portable than Basic, even though many manufacturers have added minor extensions. In machine-code and assembly-language programs originally written by someone else, be on your guard for jumps into various monitor subroutines that may not be available on your system. If you are using a monitor you may find that you will have to change the addresses of a program you take from elsewhere, as they clash with the monitor locations.

The stages in testing a coded program are:

1. Desk-checking.
2. Examining the program for textual and 'grammatical' errors such as misplaced commas and, in Basic, a FOR without a corresponding NEXT.
3. (Compiling if you are not using an interpreter.)
4. Testing each module of the program with carefully selected test data to ensure that all branches of the program are obeyed.
5. Testing the program as a whole after each module is error-free.
6. (In the case of a commercial system, some parallel running of the computer application and the system it has replaced, to ensure that it works with great amounts of data in operational conditions. In the case of a control system, such as control of heating or model railways, checking that the system works when fully connected up to the external devices.)

Desk-checking of program code

This is similar to the checking of the flowchart, except that you will be working at program instruction level, which in the case of machine code or assembly language will be at a greater level of detail than a flowchart box. You will have to keep track of the changing contents of variables, registers and stacks, and of the status of flags and interrupts. This desk-checking will save you much computer time and frustration at the actual keyboard, and should also ensure that every path in a program is followed.

Elimination of 'grammatical' errors

The examination of program statements for correctness of their *form* will economise on time later. Checking before presenting a program to the microcomputer system is especially important if you are using a compiler. Nothing is more frustrating than to have two or three attempts to compile a program faulted because of a misplaced comma, unmatched bracket or reference to a non-existent label or line number.

Text checking is especially tedious if you are using machine code and are entering it through switches rather than through a hexadecimal keyboard. You have then no alternative but to check carefully each pattern of 1s and 0s and to compare this, until you are really adept, with the appropriate pattern in the programming manual.

Until you are used to any programming language, it is as well to have constant recourse to the manual when checking for text errors. These errors are less likely to arise if you keep your statements simple and do not try to perform too many steps in a single high-level language statement. This, especially in functions, may result in an unmatched bracket.

Some common errors, in addition to those already mentioned in this section, are:

- incorrect punctuation;
- incorrect use of spaces;
- wrong form of instruction;
- opening a file more than once;
- reference to wrong device number;
- confusion between numeric 0 and alphabetic O;
- unmatched quotation marks.

The next step, if you are using a compiler or assembler, is to have your program compiled or assembled so that you can execute modules of it. During the compilation or assembly any grammatical errors that you did not correct will be indicated. If you are using an interpreter, any grammatical errors at this stage will be noticed and the appropriate error message displayed when you type RUN and attempt to execute the program.

Testing the execution of the program

At last you are seeing what the program will do. A cassette tape and a printer are invaluable attachments at this stage. The tape can hold a copy of the program that is in memory when you commence testing. Often you will make so many alterations during the testing period that you may easily forget what you started with. At the end of each testing session it is as well to take a copy of the program at that point, unless you decide that the alterations were not making any real improvement. Naturally all changes should be noted, but a tape copy of the program will keep any you forget, as 'changes to changes to changes' can sometimes occur during an inspired burst of testing at the keyboard. A printer is useful in giving you a hard copy of the program at the start and end of each testing session, and of any alterations you inserted.

Some packaged systems will detect certain errors during the running of the program when you are trying to make the system perform an impossibility. This gives rise to error messages such as:

- division by zero,
- out of data,
- non-existent file,
- overflow (result outside the maximum number that can be held).

The system will stop after displaying the error message and it is then for you to puzzle out what caused the error.

Many systems have good diagnostic aids attached to their Basic or other high-level language compiler, or to the monitor of an assembly-language or machine-code program. These can be of great assistance in determining what has happened when you get an error message, or when the results are nonsensical, or when nothing happens for such a time that you assume you have jumped into an endless loop. One system has Basic diagnostics that include:

- the listing of the values of all variables used;
- the listing of line numbers executed between stated lines — to show which path of a branch you are following, and whether you have inadvertently become caught in an endless loop.

Some monitors and development systems for machine-code and assembly-language programs provide some equivalent facilities. One system has:

- breakpoint setting — for pausing in program execution at the first (or any subsequent, at your choice) execution of a chosen instruction;
- the display of contents of registers after each instruction obeyed;
- the display of selected memory locations.

If your system does not possess the above facilities for assisting the debugging of programs, you should try and put print statements in the program to display variables and the path executed, in the case of high-level language programs. In Basic, you can identify each loop by a number and print this out each time it is obeyed. If you are testing programs at lower language levels without the aid of diagnostic facilities, you should insert instructions to print or display the contents of all registers and flags, and to print some symbol each time you execute a loop. Such statements will have to be taken out of the program, once it is tested to your satisfaction and becomes operational.

You should carefully consider, however, whether or not you are programming in a high-level language, the relevance of the items you propose to print or display: do not overload your program at the testing stage with superfluous statements.

One common diagnostic aid if you are not programming in a high-level language is the dump of the memory. This enables you, at a point when the program ceases execution, to obtain a print (if your system has a printer) of the contents of the memory (usually in hexadecimal). If you are using a Basic interpreter, you will be able to run your program a single instruction at a time so that you can see which path it is following and ascertain the contents of vital variables. Some systems for programming at a lower level (e.g. Kim) also have this feature.

During testing it is likely that you will insert amendments to the program. You should carefully note these on the copy of the code you have in front of you. The possibility that some may elude you in the heat of the moment or that you may become confused by 'changes to changes' has already been discussed when describing the advantages of obtaining a copy of the program at the end of a testing session. One of the few justifiable uses of the GO TO statement in Basic or other high-level languages is for the insertion of these possibly temporary 'patches' to your program — but when they are of proven utility you should number them in the sequence they occur. Some Basics have an automatic renumber facility to assist the insertion of *proven* or necessary alterations to a program. If you have followed the usual practice of leaving 10 vacant numbers between each line (numbering them 100, 110, 120 etc.), you will be able to insert tested patches if your system has not a renumber command. In assembly language or machine code it is advisable, if you have the memory space, to leave a page of memory free for patches; page 0 is often used for this purpose. If you are using assembly language you will probably make use of patches a great deal to avoid assembling the program frequently, especially if you can save the machine-code version on cassette tape. The NOP (no operation) instruction is useful in batches at the end of each section of a program so that amendments can replace these.

It is difficult to generalise about the faults that cause a program to fail at this stage. Some common ones are:

● Input error: 'finger trouble' is easy at the keyboard, with the result that you enter a value that will take branches of the program you never expected.
● The branches following a comparison are reversed: for instance, the coding that is intended for a branch > 12 follows the alternative path. This is easier to do than may seem apparent, especially where you have one comparison statement following another.
● A FOR statement in Basic (or its equivalent) may never reach the final value owing to an input error, logical mistake in computation, or failing to make allowance for rounding errors and differences in floating-point representation of decimal numbers (mentioned on page 48).
● A subscript to an array that exceeds the array's bounds.

Some common errors in machine-code and assembly-language programming are:

● Using the wrong instruction from the many 'add' and 'subtract' alternatives.
● Overwriting the contents of a register.
● Flag settings other than expected.
● Failing to save registers and flags when an interrupt occurs.
● Confusion between the various modes of indirect addressing.
● Scaling errors.
● Interfering with sections of Basic program, if you are using the POKE statement in mixed-language programming.

Some thought should be devoted to testing of programs that are driven by interrupts to an external control device such as an alarm or thermostat. The sections invoked by the interrupt should be rested thoroughly in isolation, with numeric data inserted in an address to simulate the action of the external device. Sometimes during the final stage of testing it is possible to construct a simple circuit with lights to represent the external device.

When you have tested the modules of the program to your satisfaction you can then run the whole program. If the program is of any length or complexity, you may well be surprised to find that, although each module is correct, there are faults when the program is run as a whole. Since you have tested the modules, the faults will lie in the passing of data from one module to another. Often erroneous assumptions about a previously-calculated value are made. This phase of testing should not take long.

If you are connecting the microcomputer to control an external device you can now take the plunge and test it out on your burglar alarms, model trains or whatever. In business data processing, after the whole program is tested you will usually find that it links with other programs in a 'suite'; e.g. a payroll program may well link up with job costing and the annual programs for tax, superannuation and national insurance totals. When a suite is first run it is usual to have a short period of parallel running with the system it replaces.

Program testing may sound laborious, but it is very stimulating to pit your wits against the microcomputer. The upkeep of the necessary documentation is rarely as time-consuming as it may appear, and if you have a cassette recorder in your system it is not at all difficult to preserve various sections of the program during testing. You will find that certain faults you make in initial programs will soon be eliminated from your style. You may find also that it is best to keep your program simple: avoid too much work in a single high-level language statement, or 'tricks' such as subtracting a value from itself to clear a register or adding two identical binary values to shift them one place left in machine-code or assembly-language statements.

You will soon gain confidence and find you are developing a 'style', in that you concentrate on using only one of the many possible ways in which certain sections of a program can be written. You will be arriving at a stage where you can read a program in a computer magazine and feel (probably with justification) that on your own microcomputer system you could do it better, faster and more economically.

Programming is essentially a creative skill, which you will find very stimulating — much more open-ended than solving crossword puzzles or even chess problems, for instance. Except for the most trivial program, no two programmers are likely to write identical programs to solve the same problem. Above all, *enjoy* your programming, and may you have the very best of luck in running all your applications smoothly.

Glossary

This is a list of terms you are likely to find used in this book and in other works dealing with the programming of microcomputer systems. It does not include terms that are related solely to the electronic construction and architecture of microcomputers and have no relevance to programming. Terms that are applicable to mainframe computers only have not been included.

Accumulator. A memory location within the computer in which data has to be stored when you wish to perform arithmetical or logical operations on it.

Address. The identifying reference of a memory location.

Array. A set of values that collectively are called by a single name. Individual values are referred to by the array name and a subscript indicating their position in the array: e.g. B(2) is the second item in array B; X(1, 4) is the fourth item on the first row of a two-dimensional array (or *matrix*) X. Lists and tables are familiar forms of an array.

ASCII. The abbreviation for American Standard Code for Information Interchange, which is the most common way of representing alphanumeric characters in binary digits inside a microcomputer system.

Assembler. A program that converts an *assembly language* program into machine code. The term is also loosely used sometimes for *assembly language* (see below).

Assembly language. A programming language that uses mnemonics to facilitate programming at the machine-code level.

BCD. Binary coded decimal. A way of expressing each decimal digit by four binary digits inside a microcomputer system.

Binary. A system of representing numbers by the two *binary digits* 1 and 0.

Binary arithmetic. Arithmetic performed on binary operands.

Bit. An abbreviation for *binary digit*.

Block. The number of items of information transferred by a single instruction from a file device such as a floppy disc or cassette tape. The term is also used for the physical area in these devices on which the data is recorded and which is separated from the next block by an *inter-block gap*.

Bug. An error in a program.

Bus. An interconnection within the microcomputer system on which data travels from one part of the system to another. The most important buses are the *data bus*, for transfers of data within the system and to and from peripherals; the *control bus*, which carries signals for system operation; and the *address bus*, which carries the 16 bits of address identification data.

Byte. A group of bits treated as a unity. It usually contains eight bits.

Chip. The silicon chip on which an integrated circuit is built.

Clock. The oscillator that generates the timing pulses for the CPU.

Compiler. The computer program that translates the *whole* of a high-level language program into machine code.

Core. Computer store or memory.

CPU. The *central processing unit*, which contains the arithmetic and logical units for performing program instructions.

Cross-assembler; cross-compiler. An assembler or compiler that translates a program, for use in a microcomputer system, on another computer – usually a minicomputer or mainframe.

Cursor. The speck of light on a VDU screen that indicates where the next character (from typing or from program instruction) will appear.

Debug. The process of eliminating programming errors.

Direct address. The standard, permanent identification of a memory location. Sometimes called an *absolute address*.

Disassembler. A program that translates machine-code programs into assembly-language instructions.

Disc (disk). A magnetically sensitive disc on which data files are stored. A microcomputer system can read data from them or write data to them.

Diskette. A small disc. Often used for a *floppy disc* (see below).

EPROM. Erasable Programmable Read-Only Memory. A part of a system memory that cannot be overwritten but can be erased (usually by ultra-violet light) and rewritten.

Field. The number of bits or bytes needed to hold a specific item of data.

Firmware. Instructions or data permanently stored.

Flag. A bit that signifies by its value (1 or 0) whether or not a certain condition (such as arithmetic overflow) is present.

Floating point. A method of representing numbers that have a fractional part. The E form in many electronic calculators.

Floppy disc. A flexible form of disc.

Flowchart. A pictorial representation of a computer program.

Hardware. The electronic and mechanical components of a microcomputer system.

Hexadecimal. A numbering system, to base 16, that uses the digits 0–9 and letters A–F (see page 21).

High-level language. A language for programming that is problem-oriented rather than machine-oriented. Uses English language and mathematical notation, which is translated into machine code by an *interpreter* or a *compiler*. Algol, Basic, Fortran, Cobol, Pascal, APL, PL/I are high-level languages.

Immediate address. The form of addressing in which an operand is stored in the command itself after the instruction code.

Indexed addressing. The form of addressing in which the direct address is found by the addition of the contents of a register (often known as an *index register*) to a value stored in the command itself.

Interface. A device, and the appropriate programs, that allows one type of electronic device (such as a peripheral) to communicate with the CPU.

Interpreter. A program that translates high-level language statements into machine code and then obeys each statement as received.

Interrupt. A signal that causes the suspension of a program under execution, in order to obey a section of program dealing with the device or condition that initiated the interrupt signal.

K. A measure of computer storage: 1024 bytes or words.

Kansas City (format). A standard for data representation on cassette tapes.

Label. An identification of a memory location.

LED. Light-emitting diode. A type of display (often found in digital watches also).

Line printer. A printer that prints a whole line at a time.

Logical instruction. An instruction that performs 'and' and 'or' operations in a microcomputer system. Sometimes used also for shifts that ignore the sign of a byte or word.

Machine code. The basic programming language that a microcomputer system can obey without an interpreter or compiler.

Mask. A pattern of bits used in logical instructions to select a particular bit pattern from a byte or word.

Memory. The part of the computer system that stores data and program instructions, which can be retrieved at high speed, independent of their location.

MPU. Microprocessor unit. The microcomputer CPU.

Object program. The machine-code program that is produced by an assembler or compiler.

Octal. A numbering system, to base 8, that uses the digits 0−7.

Operand. The address part of an instruction. This word is also used for the data used by a computer operation.

Operation code. The bits in an instruction that determine the process the instruction is to execute.

Peripheral. An input-output or file device.

Program. A set of instructions to a microcomputer system to perform a defined task.

Program counter. The register that contains the address of the next instruction to be executed.

PROM. Programmable read-only memory. A special form of ROM that can be programmed by the user.

RAM. Random-access memory. The common type of computer memory; a programmer can read or write to it and the position of a memory location does not affect the speed of retrieval.

Register. A memory location where access by the CPU is very speedy.

ROM. Read-only memory. Memory that cannot be altered by the programmer.

Software. Computer programs. Often used for those supplied from sources other than the owner of a microcomputer system.

Source program. A program that has to be translated into machine code.

Stack. A part of the memory where data is stored and retrieved on the 'last in, first out' principle.

Stack pointer. A register that defines the current location of the stack area.

Store. See *memory*.

Subroutine. A sequence of program instructions that is written once and can be called many times in a program.

VDU. Visual display unit. A television-like screen for the display of data.

Vectored interrupt. An interrupt that has a specific address for the start of the program to service it.

Word. A group of bits treated as a unity and given a single location in memory.

Suggested solutions to exercises

There are an infinite number of correct solutions to a programming problem — think of the number of alternative variables you can use in Basic alone! The order of arithmetic expressions, the order of statements and the amount of computation performed in a single statement can vary considerably, and yet each combination can come up with the correct answer. REM statements will also vary with the individual programmer.

The suggested solutions are just one possible way of solving the problems set in the exercises. All have been checked on a microcomputer system. They assume that the version of Basic you are using is not confined to integers, but they use only those instructions and functions common to the smallest versions of Basic that have standard functions and that are not confined to whole-number working. In all cases, the use of ingenious short cuts, which may well occur to you, has been avoided. No validity-checking of data inserted via an INPUT statement has been done.

Exercise 3

```
1. 100   INPUT X
   200   INPUT Y
   300   LET A = Y
   400   LET Y = X
   500   LET X = A
   600   PRINT X, Y
   700   PRINT Y, X
   9999 END
```

2. 100   INPUT N
   110   LET M = INT (N/10)
   120   LET P = N−M*10
   130   PRINT N, 10*P + M
   9999 END

3. 100   LET A = 1017
   110   LET B = 43
   120   PRINT A, B, A + B + B, A + A, B − A
   9999 END

4. 100   INPUT N
   110   PRINT "NUMBER", "SQUARE", "CUBE"
   120   PRINT N, N*N, N*N*N
   9999 END

5. 100   INPUT N
   110   LET W = INT (N/4)
   120   PRINT W, "SETS OF FOUR"
   130   PRINT N − 4*W, "LEFT OVER"
   9999 END

6. 100   INPUT L, P
   110   LET R = P/100
   120   LET Q = (1 + R)↑N
   130   PRINT (L*R*Q)/(12*(Q − 1))
   9999 END

7. 100   INPUT X, Y, C
   110   LET K = 3.141592/180
   120   LET A = C*K
   130   LET B = .5*X*Y*SIN(A)
   140   LET E = ATN (X*SIN(A)/(Y − X*COS(A)))/K
   150   LET F = ATN (Y*SIN(A)/(X − Y*COS(A)))/K
   160   LET G = SQR (X*X + Y*Y − 2X*Y*COS(A))
   170   PRINT "ANGLES =", E, F
   180   PRINT "AREA =", B
   190   PRINT "THIRD SIDE =", G
   9999 END

8. 100   INPUT R
   110   LET A = R*57.2958
   120   LET D = INT(A)
   130   LET Q = 60*(A − D)
   140   LET M = INT(Q)
   150   LET S = INT((Q − M)*60 + .5)
   160   PRINT R, "RADIANS =", D, M, S
   9999 END

Exercise 4

1. 100   LET N = 1
   110   PRINT N, N*N, N*N*N
   120   LET N = N + 1
   130   IF N < 101 THEN 110
   9999 END

```
2.  100   LET T = 0
    110   LET K = 0
    120   INPUT N
    130   LET T = T + N
    140   LET K = K + 1
    150   IF K < 10 THEN 120
    160   PRINT "AVERAGE =", T/10
    9999 END

3.  100   LET N = 2
    110   PRINT 1/N
    120   LET N = N + 1
    130   IF N < 101 THEN 110
    9999 END

4.  100   LET A = 5
    110   REM D = MKS IN 1P, F = FRANCS
    120   INPUT D, F
    130   PRINT A, A*F, A*D
    140   LET A = A + 1
    150   IF A < 101 THEN 130
    9999 END

5.  100   PRINT "A", "B", "C"
    110   LET H = 100
    120   LET M = 0
    130   PRINT (H + M)/100, (H + M + 10)/100, (H + M + 20)/100
    140   LET M = M + 20
    150   IF M < 60 THEN 130
    160   LET H = H + 100
    170   IF H < 400 THEN 120
    9999 END

6.  100   LET K = 0
    110   INPUT A, B
    120   LET H = SQR(A↑2 + B↑2)
    130   PRINT A, B, H
    140   LET K = K + 1
    150   IF K < 10 THEN 110
    9999 END

7.  100   LET P = 0
    110   LET J = 0
    120   LET K = 0
    130   LET N = 1
    140   LET T = 1
    150   LET T = SGN(T)*1/N
    160   LET P = P + T
    170   LET N = N + 2
    180   LET T = −T
    190   LET K = K + 1
    200   IF K < 100 THEN 150
    210   LET K = 0
    220   PRINT 4*P
    230   LET J = J + 1
    240   IF J < 10 THEN 150
    9999 END
```

8. 100 LET L = 0
   110 LET M = 0
   120 LET N = L + M
   130 LET L = M
   140 LET M = N
   150 IF N < 10↑3 THEN 120
   160 IF N > 10↑6 THEN 9999
   170 PRINT N
   180 GO TO 120
  9999 END

9. 100 REM MESSAGE FOR OPERATOR
   110 PRINT "ENTER SIX NUMBERS"
   120 INPUT A, B, C, P, Q, R
   130 LET D = A*Q − B*P
   140 LET E = B*R − C*Q
   150 IF D = 0 THEN 200
   160 LET X = E/D
   170 LET Y = (P*C − A*R)/D
   180 PRINT X, Y
   190 STOP
   200 IF E < > 0 THEN 230
   210 PRINT "NOT INDEPENDENT"
   220 STOP
   230 PRINT "INDETERMINATE"
  9999 END

Exercise 5.1

1. 100 FOR N = 1 TO 100
   110 PRINT N, N*N, N*N*N
   120 NEXT N
  9999 END

2. 100 LET T = 0
   110 FOR K = 1 TO 10
   120 INPUT N
   130 LET T = T + N
   140 NEXT K
   150 PRINT "AVERAGE =", T/10
  9999 END

3. 100 FOR N = 2 TO 100
   110 PRINT 1/N
   120 NEXT N
  9999 END

4. 100 REM D = MARKS IN 1P, F = FRANCS
   110 INPUT D, F
   120 FOR A = 5 TO 100
   130 PRINT A, A*F, A*D
   140 NEXT A
  9999 END

5. 100   PRINT "A", "B", "C"
   110   FOR H = 100 TO 400 STEP 100
   120   FOR M = 0 TO 60 STEP 20
   130   PRINT (H + M)/100, (H + M + 10)/100, (H + M + 20)/100
   140   NEXT M
   150   NEXT H
   9999 END

6. 100   FOR K = 1 TO 10
   110   INPUT A, B
   120   LET H = SQR(A↑2 + B↑2)
   130   PRINT A, B, H
   140   NEXT K
   9999 END

7. 100   LET N = 1
   110   LET T = 1
   120   LET P = 0
   130   FOR K = 1 TO 10
   140   FOR L = 1 TO 100
   150   LET P = SGN(T)*1/N + P
   160   LET T = –T
   170   LET N = N + 2
   180   NEXT L
   190   PRINT "AFTER", K*100, "TERMS: PI IS", 4*P
   200   NEXT K
   9999 END

Exercise 5.2

1. 100   (data list)
   110   LET T = 0
   120   DIM A(10)
   130   FOR N = 1 TO 10
   140   READ A(N)
   150   LET T = T + A(N)
   160   NEXT N
   170   LET M = T/10
   180   LET D = 0
   190   FOR J = 1 TO 10
   200   IF D > ABS(A(J) – M) THEN 230
   210   LET D = ABS(A(J) – M)
   220   LET G = A(J)
   230   NEXT J
   240   PRINT M, G
   9999 END

2. 100   DIM X(5, 3)
   110   LET B = X(1, 1)
   120   FOR I = 1 TO 5
   130   FOR J = 1 TO 3

```
140  IF X(I, J)<3 THEN 160
150  LET B = X(I, J)
160  NEXT J
170  NEXT I
180  FOR I = 1 TO 5
190  FOR J = 1 TO 3
200  LET X(I, J) = X(I, J)/B
210  NEXT J
220  NEXT I
9999 END
```

```
3.  100  DIM A(3, 4)
    110  LET B = A(1, 1)
    120  LET I = 1
    130  LET J = 1
    140  FOR K = 1 TO 3
    150  FOR L = 1 TO 4
    160  IF A(K, L) > B THEN 210
    170  NEXT L
    180  NEXT K
    190  PRINT B, I, J
    200  STOP
    210  LET I = K
    220  LET J = L
    230  LET B = A(K, L)
    240  GO TO 170
    9999 END
```

```
4.  100  DIM P(50)
    110  LET I = 1
    120  LET J = 3
    130  LET P(1) = 3
    140  LET K = 0
    150  LET K = K + 1
    160  IF P(K) <= INT(SQR(J)) THEN 230
    170  PRINT J
    180  LET P(I) = J
    190  LET I = I + 1
    200  LET J = J + 2
    210  IF J < 100 THEN 140
    220  STOP
    230  LET M = INT(J/P(K))
    240  IF J = P(K)*M THEN 200
    250  GO TO 150
    9999 END
```

```
5.  100  DIM A(10)
    110  FOR M = 1 TO 5
    120  LET A(M) = M
    130  LET A(M + 5) = M
    140  NEXT M
    150  FOR N = 0 TO 4
    160  PRINT A(N + 1), A(N + 2), A(N + 3), A(N + 4), A(N + 5)
    170  NEXT N
    9999 END
```

6. 100 (data list)
   110 LET L = 0
   120 LET M = 1000
   130 LET T = 0
   140 REM L IS LARGEST, M SMALLEST, T TOTAL
   150 LET K = 1
   160 REM K IS COUNT
   170 READ X
   180 IF X = −1 THEN 260
   190 LET T = T + X
   200 LET K = K + 1
   210 IF L > X THEN 230
   220 LET L = X
   230 IF M < X THEN 250
   240 LET M = X
   250 GO TO 170
   260 PRINT "AVERAGE", "LARGEST", "SMALLEST"
   270 PRINT T/K, L, M
 9999 END

Exercise 5.3

1. (a) 8000 LET M = INT(X/1000)
     8010 LET C = INT((X − 1000*M)/10)
     8020 LET R = X − 1000*M − 10*C
     8030 RETURN

  (b) 8000 LET Z = 0
     8010 REM Z IS TOTAL, X ARRAY, V AVERAGE
     8020 FOR Q = 1 TO 10
     8030 LET Z = Z + X(Q)
     8040 NEXT Q
     8050 LET V = Z/10
     8060 RETURN

  (c) 8000 LET Q = P
     8010 REM PRICE IN P, DISCOUNTED PRICE IN Q
     8020 IF Q > 100 THEN 8070
     8030 IF Q > 50 THEN 8050
     8040 RETURN
     8050 LET Q = .975*Q
     8060 RETURN
     8070 LET Q = .95*Q
     8080 RETURN

  (d) 8000 LET Z = E*P
     8010 REM E = RATE, P = POUNDS, $.CC IN Z
     8020 RETURN

2. 8000 LET S = A(1)
  8010 REM ARRAY IS A, SIZE IN Z
  8020 REM LARGEST IN L, SMALLEST IN S

```
     8030 LET L = A(1)
     8040 FOR Y = 2 TO Z
     8050 IF L < A(Y) THEN 8100
     8060 IF S > A(Y) THEN 8120
     8070 NEXT Y
     8080 PRINT "LARGEST IS", L, "SMALLEST IS", S
     8090 RETURN
     8100 LET L = A(Y)
     8110 GO TO 8070
     8120 LET S = A(Y)
     8130 GO TO 8070

  3. 100   INPUT N
     110   GOSUB 8000
     120   STOP
     8000 PRINT "FACTORS OF", N, "PRINTED BELOW"
     8010 DATA 2, 3, 5, 7
     8020 FOR Z = 1 TO 4
     8030 READ Y(Z)
     8040 NEXT Z
     8050 RESTORE
     8060 FOR Z = 1 TO 4
     8070 LET Q = N/Y(Z)
     8080 IF N < Q*Y(Z) THEN 8130
     8090 PRINT Y(Z)
     8100 IF Q = 1 THEN 8150
     8110 LET N = Q
     8120 GO TO 8070
     8130 NEXT Z
     8140 PRINT N
     8150 RETURN
     9999 END

  4. 8000 LET Z = B*B - 4*A*C
     8010 IF Z < > 0 THEN 8040
     8020 PRINT "ONLY 1 SOLUTION, X =", -B/2*A
     8030 RETURN
     8040 IF Z < 0 THEN 8070
     8050 PRINT "X =", (-B + SQR(Z))/2*A, "AND", (-B - SQR(Z))/2*A
     8060 RETURN
     8070 PRINT "IMAGINARY SOLUTIONS"
     8080 RETURN

  5. 8000 LET Z = A*57.2958
     8010 REM RADIANS IN A
     8020 REM DEGREES IN D, MINUTES M, SECONDS S
     8030 IF Z <= 360 THEN 8060
     8040 LET Z = Z - 360
     8050 GO TO 8030
     8060 LET D = INT(Z)
     8070 LET Z = (Z - D)*60
     8080 LET M = INT(Z)
     8090 LET S = INT((Z - M)*60 + .5)
     8100 RETURN
```

6. Exercises a–f have the following common main program:
      100 (data list of 3 items)
      110 DIM E(3)
      120 FOR I = 1 TO 3
      130 READ E(I)
      140 PRINT FNA E(I)
      150 NEXT I
      999 END

  (a)   400 DEF FNA(X) = LOG(X)/LOG(10)
  (b)   400 DEF FNA(X) = TAN(X*.0174533)
  (c)   400 DEF FNA(X) = 3.141593*X↑2
  (d)   400 DEF FNA(X) = X*.0174533
  (e)   400 DEF FNA(X) = INT(X + .5)
  (f)   400 DEF FNA(X) = X↑.3333333

Exercise 6

1. 100   data list
   110   DIM A$(5), B$(5)
   120   LET D$ = "ZZZZZZ"
   130   FOR N = 1 TO 5
   140   READ A$(N)
   150   NEXT N
   160   FOR M = 1 TO 5
   170   LET E$ = D$
   180   LET L = 1
   190   FOR N = 1 TO 5
   200   IF A$(N) >= E$ THEN 220
   210   LET E$ = A$(N)
   220   LET L = N
   230   NEXT N
   240   LET A$(L) = D$
   250   LET B$(M) = E$
   260   NEXT M
   270   FOR K = 1 TO 5
   280   PRINT B$(K)
   290   NEXT K
   9999 END

2. 100   INPUT N
   110   DATA "ZERO", "ONE", "TWO", "THREE", "FOUR"
   120   DATA "FIVE", "SIX", "SEVEN", "EIGHT", "NINE"
   130   DATA "TEN"
   140   DIM X$(11)
   150   FOR K = 1 TO 11
   160   READ X$(K)
   170   NEXT K
   180   LET R = N – 11*INT(N/11)
   190   PRINT X$(R + 1)
   9999 END

3. 100 (data list)
   ```
   110  FOR L = 1 TO 10
   120  READ N
   130  PRINT N,
   140  FOR M = 1 TO 10
   150  PRINT "+";
   160  NEXT M
   170  PRINT
   180  NEXT L
   9999 END
   ```

4. ```
   100  REM CLEAR COUNTERS 1–6
   110  DIM N(6)
   120  FOR K = 1 TO 6
   130  LET N(K) = 0
   140  NEXT K
   150  FOR M = 1 TO 100
   160  LET X = INT(6*RND(1)) + 1
   170  LET N(X) = N(X) + 1
   180  NEXT M
   190  REM PRINTS COUNTS 1–6
   200  FOR K = 1 TO 6
   210  PRINT N(K)
   220  NEXT K
   9999 END
   ```

5. ```
   100  REM RANDOM NO. SHOWS VALUE OF SUITS ARE
   110  REM HTS 1–13; DIA 14–26; CLUBS 27–39; SP 40–52
   120  REM SO THAT 7 CLUBS = 33
   130  FOR K = 1 TO 13
   140  LET X = INT(52*RND(1)) + 1
   150  REM CALCULATE SUIT INDICATOR
   160  LET A = INT(X/13.3)
   170  LET B = X – 13*A
   180  REM B IS POSITION IN SUIT
   190  IF B = 1 THEN 30
   200  IF B = 12 THEN 320
   210  IF B = 13 THEN 340
   220  IF B = 11 THEN 360
   230  PRINT B, "OF"
   240  IF A = 0 THEN 380
   250  IF A = 1 THEN 400
   260  IF A = 2 THEN 420
   270  PRINT "SPADES"
   280  NEXT K
   290  STOP
   300  PRINT "ACE OF"
   310  GO TO 240
   320  PRINT "QUEEN OF"
   330  GO TO 240
   340  PRINT "KING OF"
   350  GO TO 240
   360  PRINT "JACK OF"
   370  GO TO 240
   ```

```
380  PRINT "HEARTS"
390  GO TO 280
400  PRINT "DIAMONDS"
410  GO TO 280
420  PRINT "CLUBS"
430  GO TO 280
9999 END
```

```
6. 100  PRINT "PAIR", "IMPAIR", "MANQUE", "PASSE"
   110  REM CLEAR COUNTERS
   120  LET A = 0
   130  LET B = 0
   140  LET C = 0
   150  LET D = 0
   160  FOR K = 1 TO 1000
   170  LET X = INT(36*RND(1)) + 1
   180  IF X < 19 THEN 250
   190  LET D = D + 1
   200  IF X − 2*INT(X/2) = 0 THEN 270
   210  LET B = B + 1
   220  NEXT K
   230  PRINT A, B, C, D
   240  STOP
   250  LET C = C + 1
   260  GO TO 200
   270  LET A = A + 1
   280  GO TO 220
   9999 END
```

Index